The Essential Gluten Free

Cookie Guide

Learn how to make chocolate chip, sugar, snickerdoodle
treats plus more than 50 other recipes

Brianna Hobbs

The Essential Gluten-Free Cookie Guide
by Brianna Hobbs

Copyright ©2014 by Triumph Dining
http://www.triumphdining.com

ISBN: 978-1-61431-028-0 Paperback, monochrome $16.95
ISBN: 978-1-61431-029-7 Paperback, color $21.95
ISBN: 978-1-61431-033-4 Hardcover $24.95

Book cover design by Jeff Weeks
Interior design and layout by Val Sherer, Personalized Publishing Services

Triumph Dining
144 Diablo Ranch Court, Danville, CA 94506 USA

Table of Contents

Chapter 1

Basic Information

Why measure by weight instead of volume?

Yes, that probably isn't how Mom used to do it so let me tell you why you should measure by weight; It is a much more accurate way of measuring things like flour. Depending on how you scoop flour and how much air is in the flour, the same cup full could differ more than an ounce in weight. How can that extra flour affect your cookies? Too much or too little flour blend can entirely change the texture of your cookie. Too much flour and the cookie will be dry and crumbly, too little flour and the cookie will spread far too thin and will lack the necessary structure.

If you have to measure by volume it is very important that you measure consistently, and the same way that I did while developing all of these recipes.

If you have to measure flour by volume use a spoon to scoop the flour into the measuring cup, and then level it off using a butter knife or the back of your finger.

Brown sugar is also a little tricky, the most accurate way to measure it is to *firmly* pack it into the measuring cup.

If there is a weight measurement for an ingredient, then use it if you can. Some ingredients I've found easier to measure by volume instead of weight, like peanut butter, baking soda, salt, or xanthan gum, so there will only be volume measurements for those ingredients.

My GF Cookie Blend

I've developed my own gluten-free blend that I like to use in all of my cookie and cake recipes. This flour blend doesn't work well for pasta or bread doughs, but that isn't what this cookbook is all about. My blend is:

1 part white rice flour
1 part brown rice flour
1 part potato starch
1 part tapioca starch or flour

Let me tell you why I love my flour blend, and what makes it different than other blends. I have found in baking cookies that I prefer working with a flour blend that has more starch in it, compared to a traditional blend. My blend is 50% starches, and 50% rice flours, which I have found prevents the typical sandy and gritty texture that is often found in gluten-free baked goods. The other reason I love my flour blend is the fine and soft texture that it lends to the finished baked goods. My flour blend is more like a wheat "cake flour" having less protein, and more starch instead of the typical all purpose flour that has more protein than starch. So when using my GF Cookie Blend think of it as your new favorite cake flour, perfect for all of your baked goods.

If desired, you can use 2 parts of white rice, or brown rice, instead of the 1 part of each. In my experience it really only affects the color of the finished baked goods, and the nutritional value, but not the texture of the finished product.

Make sure to use potato starch, not potato flour. They are NOT the same thing. However, tapioca starch and tapioca flour are basically the same. Be careful not to mix them up. If you were to use potato flour your cookies would not turn out right.

If you prefer to use a different all-purpose rice-based gluten-free flour blend in these recipes feel free to experiment. I'd be careful using any flour blend NOT based on rice flour, and please do NOT use a bean flour based blend. The proteins in the bean flours are very different and the finished cookies often come out with funky flavors (don't even think about tasting the dough, bleck!) The finished product may have a different texture depending on the proportions of the flours that are in the blend that you use. Of course, I recommend my blend as that is what I've tested all my recipes with.

Butter

Many of my recipes use butter. In some of the recipes it is melted, in other recipes it is softened. Melted butter is great for helping cookies to be chewy, which is why I use it. If I say to melt the butter, melt it. It makes those cookies so much better. There are still lots of recipes that call for softened butter, melted butter doesn't always work better, so just make sure you pay attention and use the butter that is called for in the recipe.

If you can't have dairy, don't worry there are some great options for you! I'd suggest using earth balance sticks, or your favorite butter substitute. Coconut oil is good too.

The taste will not be quite the same, there really is nothing the same as butter, but the cookies will still be delicious, and should have the same texture. I recommend using a refined coconut oil, a virgin or unrefined oil will have a strong flavor that may come through in your cookie. Just be sure that you substitute is in the same "state" as the butter called for in the recipe, softened or melted.

Eggs

You may notice that in some of my recipe only the egg yolk is called for. The egg yolk alone doesn't have excess moisture and will result in a chewier cookie. If a recipe calls for only the yolk, please don't use a whole egg. The cookie will spread too much, and will have a very different texture.

If you can't have eggs a great substitute is a "Chia Egg." If you've read through the recipe for Aunt Joanne's Fire Cookies you may have noticed the ground chia seeds mixed with water in that recipe that acts as an egg substitute . For each "egg" mix together 1 tablespoon ground chia seed and 2 tablespoons water. Mix quickly because it gels up pretty fast. This is a great substitution for whole eggs and should work in most of my recipes calling for whole eggs. They won't work the same in my recipes that call for only the yolk, or only the white.

Baking Soda and Baking Powder

Baking soda helps cookies to rise and spread. Baking powder helps cookies to rise. Don't mix them up, and you'll need both. Different recipes call for baking powder, or soda, because they react differently in those batters. You really can't substitute them for each other.

Xanthan gum

Not the same thing as Guar Gum, Xanthan gum is a fine powder that you can buy online, or in the gluten-free section of many grocery stores. It is essential in the recipes that call for it. Xanthan gum is commonly used in gluten-free baking to replace the structure of gluten in traditional baked goods. Without it your cookie will crumble apart, so don't skip it even if it is only ¼ teaspoon. It is essential!

Salt

You don't taste when it is there, only when it isn't. I just use plain table salt when I'm baking but it really doesn't make a difference what salt you use, as long as you use it.

Brown and White Sugar

Some of the recipes call for brown sugar, and others for white. I use both all the time and don't recommend substituting them for each other. Brown sugar adds just a little extra moisture and color too cookies, and normally produces a chewier cookie. White sugar makes cookies more crisp, and also helps to avoid the additional color when you are making sugar or other white cookies. You can easily make your own brown sugar by stirring a little molasses (probably about 1-2 tablespoons per cup) into some white sugar.

Powdered Sugar

Most often I use powdered sugar (or confectioner's sugar) in frostings and toppings, but occasionally I do use it in a dough recipe because it creates a very fine and smooth texture like in my snowball cookies. Be sure to use powdered sugar when it is called for. In a pinch you can make your own "superfine" sugar by processing white sugar in a blender or food processor until it is powdery. It will work fine for doughs, but if you make any frostings with your superfine sugar they will be a bit gritty.

Cocoa Powder

I tested all of my recipes with plain old cocoa powder. I guess I'm not fancy enough to play around with the dutch-processed cocoa powder. Either will work just fine in my recipes. The flavor of the dutch-processed cocoa is more rounded (some even say more chocolatey.) The texture of your cookies should be the same, no matter which cocoa you use.

Oats

I normally buy old-fashioned rolled oats. If you need quick oats, like in my Oatmeal Creme Pies, simply pulse the oats in your food processor or blender for a few seconds.. Make sure that your oats come from a reliable gluten-free source. Oats are gluten-free by nature, but are often cross-contaminated with wheat when processed.

Chocolate Chips

Chocolate chips are normally "safe" but if you are very sensitive check with the manufacturer to make sure that there isn't any cross-contamination in their facilities. I use chocolate chips all the time, in MANY of my recipes. You can also use coarsely chopped chocolate bars if you prefer. I really recommend using a candy coating or almond bark for dipping or drizzling melted chocolate on baked cookies. It sets up much quicker than melted chocolate and is easier to handle. You can use melted chocolate instead but you may need to help the chocolate set by popping your cookies in the freezer for a few minutes.

Peanut Butter

I'm a big fan of Peanut Butter, and there are several peanut butter cookie recipes in here. If you don't like PB or have an allergy you should be able to substitute any other nut butter that you'd like.

Oil

In most recipes I just used a vegetable based cooking oil. You probably have some sort of cooking oil in your kitchen, I just prefer using a light tasting oil in most of my cookies. If you use a stronger oil (like coconut or olive oil) I suggest using a refined version of that oil and not virgin. The flavor is more subtle and will blend into the cookie more easily.

Almond Flour

Only a few of these recipes have almond flour in them, but they are worth the special purchase. Almond flour is the base in my Dark Chocolate Brownies (which I think just might be my favorite brownie recipe in this book.) It texturally contributes in ways that no other flour could.

Chia Seeds

I don't use Chia Seeds very often, but if you have a sensitivity to eggs then you'll definitely want to get some (see "Chia Egg in the egg section.) They are pretty readily available at health food stores and some supermarkets. If you can't find them near you then turn to the internet.

Extracts & Spices

You really have to have vanilla extract in your kitchen, no way around it. I also use almond extract in several of my recipes, it really helps to round out the flavor of those cookies and they just aren't the same without it. I love peppermint extract too, but I only use it in my Peppermint Soft Frosted Sugar Cookies. You also need ground cinnamon, ground nutmeg, ground ginger, ground clove, and chili powder. Chili powder is my secret weapon, it adds really adds depth to some chocolate and spice cookies.

Sprinkles and Food Coloring

They really are just for fun. If you are opposed to food coloring then just skip them.

SUPPLIES

The Basics

You can't do much baking without a few mixing bowls, spatulas, spoons, a whisk, measuring cups, or measuring spoons. You don't need anything too fancy, but you have to have the basics.

Stand or Handheld Mixer

I love my stand mixer. I highly recommend using a mixer anytime the instruction is given to "cream" ingredients, especially if the butter is softened. In a recipe that calls for melted butter it is normally pretty easy to mix by hand, but I still use my stand mixer especially if I'm making a larger batch. If you need to cream softened butter and don't have a stand mixer I suggest using a sturdy hand held version, which you can normally purchase for $20-40.

An electric mixer of some sort is ESSENTIAL for making frostings. You have to beat the butter for a minimum of 3 minutes, normally 5, with an electric mixer to incorporate enough air to have a fluffy frosting. You really can't get the same result by hand.

Electronic Scale

You don't need anything too fancy; I recommend digital; it is what I use and what I've found to be easiest and most widely available. The functions that you want to make sure it has is the ability to weigh in ounces (and switch to pounds and grams too), and a tare feature. The tare will let you zero out your measuring bowl, and other ingredients in the bowl which means you aren't constantly doing math in your head. Without a tare feature it is very easy to make mistakes in measuring. It is also nice if your scale is big enough that you can still see the display with a mixing bowl on the scale. Mine isn't that big, so I have to measure the ingredients individually and then dump them in my mixing bowl. If you plan on doing your measuring in your mixing bowl, make sure that your scale can weigh up to 11 pounds instead of 2 pounds or 5 pounds, when you have all the ingredients in the bowl a smaller scale won't suffice. I don't see the point in forking out too much money on a fancy scale, you should be able to get an affordable one for $20-$40. It is well worth the investment!

Silicone Baking Mats
I absolutely love my silicone baking mats! With it, clean up is a breeze and cookies never stick. My husband got me a set of 2 for Christmas about a year ago, and I use them all the time! They are by far one of my favorite kitchen tools. My mats aren't the popular name brand but they cost half as much. Best $20 my hubby spent!

Parchment Paper
Parchment paper is another must-have around the kitchen. Use it to line your baking sheets if you don't have a silicone baking mat. I always use it to line my 8" x 8" or 9" x 13"

when I'm making bar cookies or brownies. It makes removing the baked bars super easy. To line a baking sheet just press a square of parchment paper down into the baking dish before spreading or pressing the batter. When the bars are done you just lift the parchment paper up and the bars come with it.

Cookie Scoop
Using a cookie scoop or spring loaded disher helps to ensure that all of the cookies are portioned evenly, which means they will all finish baking at the same time. It also saves lots of time, being much faster than scooping out dough and rolling it by hand. Most of the recipes in this book use a 1½ tablespoon scoop, so make sure you have one on hand. I used a bigger scoop for a few recipes, but you will only use those scoops if you are making really big cookies. So unless you're a fan of big cookies, save your storage space and only buy a 1½ tablespoon scoop.

Baking Sheets
Also called cookies sheets, whichever you call them, you'll need a few. I like having at least 2 on hand for making cookies, that way you can switch them out, baking one sheet at a time while you load the other up with dough.

8" x 8" and 9" x 13" Baking Pans
Mine are glass but you can also use metal, you just may need to adjust the baking time.

Baby Bent Spatula

I love my small offset spatula, it makes frosting cookies or bars, or spreading batter out evenly in a pan super easy. If you don't have one you can make do without, but it is a small investment to make if you bake often.

Piping Bag, Tips, and Plastic Bags

I love all my tips, but the only one you really need for making cookies is a really big round one. You can probably make do without using any tips, and just the coupler and the bag. Using a bag makes frosting cut out cookies a breeze; getting an even layer of frosting with much less mess. I often use plastic gallon size bags when piping frosting instead. Just cut off a small bit of plastic from a corner and then drop your tip in (if you are using a tip) before you load in the frosting. They make cleanup a breeze, just toss them when you are done.

I like using sandwich sized plastic bags when dealing with melted chocolate or almond bark. Just cut a tiny little bit of plastic off of the corner after you fill the bag with chocolate. I don't like using a tip and piping bag for chocolate because I've found that as the chocolate cools a little bit, any unmelted bits clog the tip and make it impossible to squeeze any chocolate out. The plastic bag gives the flexibility that is necessary. Also, once the chocolate cools, it can be tricky to clean out of a piping bag; with a sandwich bag you avoid clean-up entirely.

Sieve

Most often I use it to dust powdered sugar on finished cookies, but it is a useful tool to have in the kitchen.

Cookie Cutters

I have a set of rounds in lots of different sizes, those are the cutters I use the most. I also like to have a gingerbread man, heart, and a flower on hand, but get whatever shapes you like. Stars, trains, animals, etc. They are all fun! I have found that using cutters with smaller intricate edges make it difficult to keep my sugar cookies soft, like stars with long points or intricate snowflakes. While they are still beautiful and tons of fun, they are much crisper cookies so I stick to big shapes whenever possible.

Chapter 2

Traditional Cookies

Flourless Peanut Butter Cookies

These little gems are just packed with peanut butter. Chewy and sweet they are my most favorite peanut butter cookie, and no flour means that they are easy for even an unseasoned gluten-free baker to whip up.

Yield: 16 cookies

Directions:

1. Preheat oven to 350 degrees F. Line baking sheets with parchment paper or silicone baking mats.

2. Mix together the peanut butter, sugar, egg, and salt until smooth.

3. Scoop using a 1½ tablespoon cookie scoop and place 2-3 inches apart on the lined baking sheets.

4. Flatten each cookie using the tines of a fork to make a cross-hatch pattern.

5. Bake for 8-10 minutes. Cool for a few minutes on the baking sheet before moving to a cooling rack to finish cooling.

Ingredients:

1 cup peanut butter

6 ounces (¾ cup) white sugar

1 egg

¼ teaspoon salt

Flourless Triple Chocolate Cookies

Rich, full of gooey melted chocolate, soft, and chewy, these will easily become your favorite chocolate cookie. Most kitchens (even typical non-gluten-free kitchens) will probably already have everything on hand to make these right away.

Yield: About 1½ dozen

DIRECTIONS:

1. Preheat your oven to 350 degrees F. Line your baking sheets with parchment paper or a silicone baking mat.

2. In your stand mixer, cream together the butter and sugar. Add the egg and mix until combined. Add the vanilla, salt, baking soda, and cocoa powder, and mix until you have a smooth dough. Reserve approximately 2 tablespoons of each of the white and chocolate chips for pressing in the tops of the cookies. Stir in the rest of the chocolate chips until distributed throughout.

3. Scoop the dough using a 1½ tablespoon cookie scoop and drop 3 inches apart on your baking sheets. Bake for approximately 10 minutes. They will lose their doughy shine on the top but will still be very soft when they are done.

4. Immediately after they come out of the oven press a few of the reserved white and chocolate chips into the tops of the cookies.

5. Allow to cool on the baking sheet for several minutes to allow the cookies to firm up before moving to a cooling rack.

INGREDIENTS:

4 ounces (½ cup) butter, softened

4 ounces (1 cup) powdered sugar

1 egg

1 teaspoon vanilla

½ teaspoon baking soda

½ teaspoon salt

4 ounces (1 cup) cocoa powder

3 ounces (½ cup) white chocolate chips, divided

3.5 ounces (½ cup) milk, semisweet, or dark chocolate chips, divided

Chocolate Oatmeal Raisin

Classic, chewy, oatmeal cookies with just a hint of honey and cinnamon. When I was a little girl oatmeal cookies were one of my favorites; I didn't like raisins, though, so I always used chocolate chips instead. My husband feels the same way about raisins, so we only do chocolate chips at our house. I send the raisin ones over to my mom; she loves them!

Yield: About 20 cookies

DIRECTIONS:

1. Preheat the oven to 350 degrees F. Line a baking sheet with parchment paper or a silicone baking mat.

2. Cream together the melted butter and brown sugar. Add the eggs and mix until combined. Add the baking soda, salt, xanthan gum, honey, cinnamon, and vanilla and mix until combined.

3. Add the flour and oats and mix until incorporated (first at low speed and then turn the speed up.) Then mix in the chocolate chips or raisins.

4. Scoop using a 1½ tablespoon cookie scoop and place cookies 2-3 inches apart on the prepared baking sheet.

5. Bake for approximately 10 minutes. The cookies will spread and will lose their doughy shine, but will still be very soft when they are done. Allow to cool on the baking sheet for a few minutes before moving to a cooling rack to finish cooling.

INGREDIENTS:

4 ounces (½ cup) butter, melted

5.5 ounces (¾ cup + 2 tablespoons firmly packed) brown sugar

2 egg YOLKS

½ teaspoon xanthan gum

½ teaspoon salt

½ teaspoon baking soda

1 teaspoon vanilla

½ teaspoon cinnamon

1 tablespoon honey

11 ounces (2 cups) GF Cookie Blend

3 ounces (¾ cup) rolled GF oats

6 ounces (1 cup) chocolate chips OR 5 ounces (1 cup) raisins

Snickerdoodle Cookies

Soft and chewy cookies coated in a sweet, cinnamon-sugar coating, snickerdoodles were always a favorite of mine when I was a child. They are well worth the extra work of rolling the dough into balls and coating them in the cinnamon sugar. I didn't always have the patience to do it when I was younger, and if you don't either try just scooping the dough and sprinkling it with the cinnamon sugar instead. My little twist on the classic flavor profile is just a pinch of nutmeg. I love the little hint of spiciness it lends, rounding out the flavor. If you don't like nutmeg you can just omit it.

DIRECTIONS:

1. Cream the butter and sugar together. Add the eggs and beat until combined.

2. Add the salt, baking powder, cinnamon, xanthan gum, and vanilla. Then add the GF Cookie Blend and mix until combined.

3. Cover the bowl of your mixer in plastic wrap and chill the cookie dough for at least 1 hour. (If you don't want to bake your cookies today, seal the dough in an airtight container or freezer bag and freeze up to 2-3 months.)

4. When your dough is chilled and you are ready to bake, preheat the oven to 350 degrees F.

5. Mix together the spices and sugar. Drop the dough into sugar mixture using a 1½ tablespoon cookie scoop and roll around until well coated. Place the sugar coated dough on a parchment or silicone baking mat lined baking sheet and flatten slightly, either using the bottom of a glass dipped in the sugar spice mixture, or the heel of your hand.

6. Bake in your pre-heated oven for 10-12 minutes. They will still be soft but the edges will just start to look dry, and the bottom of the cookie will just be starting to brown. Let cool for 5-10 minutes on the baking sheet, and then remove to a cooling rack.

INGREDIENTS:

6 ounce (¾ cup) butter, softened

12 ounces (1½ cup) sugar

3 eggs

1 teaspoon salt

½ teaspoon ground cinnamon

2 ¼ teaspoon baking powder

2¼ teaspoon xanthan gum

2 ¼ teaspoon vanilla

27 ounces (4 ¾ cup + 1 tablespoon) GF Cookie Blend

TOPPING:

approximately 1 cup sugar

1 teaspoon ground cinnamon

¼ teaspoon ground nutmeg

Monster Cookies

• •

Monster Cookies were the big thing online a few years ago. Crispy, peanut butter and oatmeal cookies with candy coated chocolate and chocolate chips. Kids love them! (And grown-ups too.)

Yield: 20-24 cookies

DIRECTIONS:

1. Preheat oven to 350 degrees F. Line a baking sheet with parchment paper or a silicone baking mat.

2. Beat together all ingredients except for the rolled oats, M&Ms and chocolate chips until very fluffy. Add the remaining ingredients and scoop using a 1½ tablespoon cookie scoop and place 2-3 inches apart on the baking sheet.

3. Bake for 10-12 minutes

4. Allow to cool on the baking sheet for a few minutes before moving to a cooling rack to finish cooling.

INGREDIENTS:

2 eggs

4 ounces (½ cup) brown sugar, firmly packed

⅔ cup white sugar

½ teaspoon vanilla

2.5 ounces (5 tablespoons) butter

1 cup peanut butter

1½ teaspoon baking soda

9 ounces (3 cups) rolled oats, GF

5 ounces (⅔ cup) chocolate chips

5 ounces (⅔ cup) candy coated chocolate or peanut butter candies (like M&Ms or Reeses Pieces)

¼ cup plus 2 tablespoons milk

White Chocolate Macadamia

I love the sweet nuttiness that the macadamia nuts give these cookies. The white chocolate pairs so well with them. Chewy, soft, sweet, these are the best white chocolate macadamia nut cookies that I've had!

Yield: About 2 dozen cookies

Directions:

1. Preheat the oven to 350 degrees F.. Line a baking sheet with parchment paper or a silicone baking mat.

2. Cream together the melted butter and sugar. Add the egg yolks and mix until combined. Add the baking soda, salt, xanthan gum, and vanilla and mix until combined.

3. Add the GF Cookie Blend and mix until incorporated. Then mix in the white chocolate chips and nuts.

4. Scoop using a 1½ tablespoon cookie scoop and place cookies 2-3 inches apart on the prepared baking sheet.

5. Bake for 10 minutes. The cookies should spread and will lose their doughy shine, but will still be very soft. Allow to cool on the baking sheet for a few minutes before moving to a cooling rack to finish cooling.

Ingredients:

4 ounces (½ cup) butter, melted

5.5 ounces (¾ cup) sugar

2 egg YOLKS

½ teaspoon xanthan gum

½ teaspoon baking soda

1 teaspoon vanilla

9 ounces (1½ cups) GF Cookie Blend

6 ounces (1 cup) white chocolate chips

2 ounces (½ cup) macadamia nuts, toasted and chopped

Pecan Sandies

* *

These traditional southern cookies are sweet and nutty. It's a soft cookie with crispy edges and it isn't overly sweet. Using powdered sugar in the dough helps the cookie to have a very fine texture and a smooth mouthfeel.

Yield: 1 dozen

Directions:

1. Cream the butter and sugar together. Add the egg and beat until combined.

2. Add the salt, xanthan gum, and vanilla . Then add the GF Cookie Blend and mix until combined. Add the chopped pecans and mix until they are evenly distributed throughout.

3. Chill for at least an hour before baking.

4. When your dough is chilled and you are ready to bake preheat oven to 350 degrees F. Line your baking sheets with parchment paper or a silicone baking mat.

5. Scoop the dough using a 1½ tablespoon cookie scoop and place 3 inches apart on the baking sheet. Gently press a whole pecan half on the top of each cookie. Bake for 12-14 minutes or until the cookie loses its doughy shine and sets up slightly, and the bottom turns a nice golden brown. Cool on the baking sheet for a few minutes before moving to a cooling rack to finish cooling.

Ingredients:

2 ounces (¼ cup) butter

4 ounces (1 cup) powdered sugar

1 egg

5.5 ounce(1 cup) GF Cookie Blend

¼ teaspoon xanthan gum

2 ounces (½ cup) pecans, chopped

1 teaspoon vanilla

¼ teaspoon salt

12 pecan halves, for garnishing

Soft Frosted Sugar Cookies

These sugar cookies are soft, cakey, and not overly sweet. They are a dead ringer for those round pink frosted cookies in the clear plastic clamshells, you know, those ones. I tried for ages to may a copy cat version of those cookies and I finally have it. I have an older version of this recipe on my blog, but I am very excited to share my new and improved recipe with you. The dough is easier to work with, plus I've mastered the techniques for making these cookies much easier to frost and cut out. You get all my tips and short cuts!

Yield: 2½-3 dozen cookies

Directions:

1. Cream the butter and sugar together on low-medium speed. Add the eggs and beat until combined.

2. Add the salt, baking powder, xanthan gum, and vanilla. Then add the GF Cookie Blend and mix until combined.

3. Cover the bowl of your mixer in plastic wrap and chill the cookie dough for at least 1 hour. (If you don't to bake your cookies today, seal the dough in an airtight container or freezer bag and freeze up to 2-3 months.)

4. When your dough is chilled and you are ready to bake preheat the oven to 350 degrees F.

5. Lay your silicone baking mat or a sheet of parchment paper on the countertop. Place dough on top, and then place another sheet of parchment on top. Roll the dough out between the parchment or silicone baking mats until it is ½ inch thick. Peel off the top sheet and cut the cookies out using a 3-3½ inch round cookie cutter, leaving at least 2 inches between the cookies. DO NOT take the cookies off of the baking mat or bottom piece of parchment, you will be baking them just like that. Not taking them off prevents the dough from stretching out of shape. Peel the excess dough off and re-roll the same way, onto a new baking mat or sheet of parchment.

6. Bake in your pre-heated oven for 8-10 minutes. They will still be soft but the edges will just start to look dry, and the bottom of the cookie will just be starting to brown. Let cool for 5-10 minutes on the baking sheet, and then remove to a cooling rack.

7. Alternatively, drop the dough onto prepared baking sheet using a 1½ tablespoon cookie scoop and us the bottom of a glass dipped in white sugar to press the cookie out so that is it about 3 inches across. So easy and no roll. The extra sugar adds a pleasant crunch too. If you were to use colored sugar no added decorations would be needed.

Frost with *American Buttercream*

Ingredients:

6 ounces (¾ cup) butter, softened

12 ounces (1½ cup) sugar

3 eggs

1 teaspoon salt

2¼ teaspoon baking powder

2¼ teaspoon xanthan gum

2 ¼ teaspoon vanilla

27 ounces (4¾ cup + 1 tablespoon) GF Cookie Blend

Filling

3 X batch of *American Buttercream*, page 139

Giant Chewy Chocolate Chip Cookies

This is the ultimate gluten-free chocolate chip cookie recipe. Buttery, chewy, soft, and packed with chocolate. These bakery-style cookies are more like a meal; they are almost as big as your head. Once you master this recipe you can use the dough as a base for creating almost any flavor of cookie you'd like.

Yield: 7 really, really big cookies (can easily double if you want more)

Directions:

1. Preheat the oven to 350 degrees F. Line a baking sheet with parchment paper or a silicone baking mat.

2. Cream together the melted butter and brown sugar on medium-low speed. Add the eggs and mix until combined. Add the baking soda, salt, xanthan gum, and vanilla and mix until combined.

3. Add the flour, and mix until incorporated. Then mix in the chocolate chips

4. Scoop using a #12 scoop (5 tablespoons) and place cookies 4 inches apart on the prepared baking sheet. (5 or 6 to a sheet.)

5. Bake for 15 minutes. The cookies should spread and will lose their doughy shine, but will still be very soft. Allow to cool on the baking sheet for a few minutes before moving to a cooling rack to finish cooling.

Ingredients:

- 4 ounces (½ cup) butter, melted
- 5.5 ounces (½ cup + 3 tablespoons firmly packed) brown sugar
- 2 egg YOLKS
- ½ teaspoon xanthan gum
- ½ teaspoon baking soda
- 1 teaspoon vanilla
- 9 ounces (1½ cups plus 2 tablespoons) GF Cookie Blend
- 6 ounces (1 cup) chocolate chips

Gingerbread Cut-Outs

No cookie collection is complete without a traditional gingerbread cut-out. These are simple and easy to make. Don't be scared of royal icing, it is actually very simple to make and frosts the cookies with smooth and shiny designs. It is perfect for applying sprinkles or gluing together a gingerbread house. If you are using this dough to make your gingerbread houses, just bake the cookies for 10 minutes instead of 8 for a crisper, sturdier cookie (bigger house pieces may need a little longer.)

Yield: About 3 dozen cut-outs

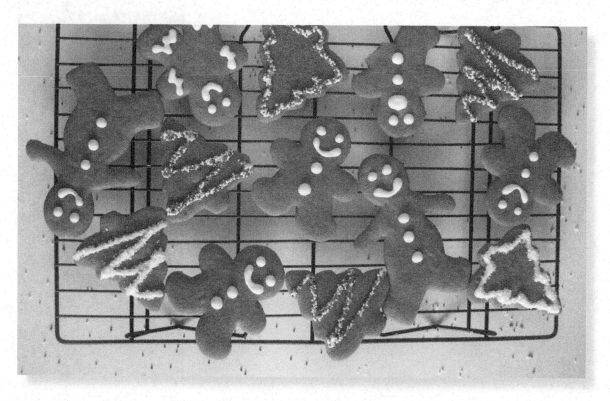

DIRECTIONS:

1. Cream together the brown sugar and shortening. Add the egg and molasses and mix until smooth. Add all the remaining ingredients and mix on until a smooth dough is formed.

2. Chill dough for at least an hour in the fridge, up to 2-3 days (if you want to wait longer to bake the cookies I suggest storing the dough in the freezer and then letting it thaw in the fridge for several hours before rolling.)

3. Preheat the oven to 350 degrees F. Line baking sheets with parchment paper or silicone baking mats.

4. Divide the dough in half and roll the dough out between 2 sheets of plastic wrap until it is ¼ inch thick. Cut out with desired cookie cutters and place half and inch apart on prepared baking sheet and bake for approximately 8 minutes. The cookie will be done when it loses its doughy shine, but it will still be soft if you touch it.

5. Cool for a few minutes on the baking sheet before moving to a cooling rack to finish cooling.

6. Repeat with remaining cookies.

7. Frost with **Royal Icing** (or *Buttercream*) if desired and decorate with sprinkles.

INGREDIENTS:

7.5 ounces (¾ cup) brown sugar, firmly packed

3.5 ounces (½ cup) shortening

1 egg

½ cup molasses

¾ teaspoon baking powder

½ teaspoon salt

1 teaspoon xanthan gum

1 teaspoon ground ginger

¾ teaspoon ground cinnamon

¼ teaspoon ground nutmeg

¼ teaspoon ground clove

16.5 ounces (3 cup) GF Cookie Blend

Royal Icing, page 144

Chapter 3

Twisted drops

Pumpkin Chocolate Chip

When I was a little girl, one of my favorite things to make with my mom was pumpkin chocolate chip muffins. I love that these cookies have all the same flavors but instead tasting like a cakey muffin top, they have that nice cookie chew. The secret is that the pumpkin acts as an egg replacer.

Yield: About 1½ dozen cookies

DIRECTIONS:

1. Cream together the melted butter and both sugars. Add the vanilla and the pumpkin and mix to combine. Add all the remaining ingredients (except the chocolate chips) and mix until all the flour is incorporated. Stir in the chocolate chips. Chill the dough for at least 30 minutes before baking (up to 3 days).

2. Preheat the oven to 350 degrees F. Line your baking sheet with parchment paper or a silicone baking mat.

3. Scoop your chilled dough onto the baking sheet about 3 inches apart using a 1½ tablespoon cookie scoop. Flatten each scoop slightly with the palm of your hand.

4. Bake for 8-10 minutes or until the cookies lose their doughy shine and look set around the edges. The cookies will still be very soft when they are finished baking. Allow them to cool for a few minutes before removing them from the baking sheet to finish cooling on a cooling rack. They will set up more as they cool.

Recipe adapted from Sally McKenney of Sally's Baking Addiction

INGREDIENTS:

4 ounces (½ cup) butter, melted

2 ounces (¼ cup) brown sugar, firmly packed

4 ounces (½ cup) white sugar

1 teaspoon vanilla

6 tablespoons canned pureed 100 % pumpkin

8.25 ounces (1½ cup) GF Cookie Blend

½ teaspoon xanthan gum

¼ teaspoon salt

¼ teaspoon baking powder

¼ teaspoon baking soda

1½ teaspoon cinnamon

½ teaspoon nutmeg

3 ounces (½ cup) chocolate chips

S'mores Cookies

....

I think that the only thing better than a S'more is a S'more made with a big chewy chocolate chip cookie. Every summer since I was a teenager my family has gone camping at a lake with a bunch of friends; now my husband and daughter come too. Last year I had made a bunch of cookies to sell at the farmer's markets, and then wasn't able to make it to the market to sell them. I had almost 30 of my Giant Chewy Chocolate Chip Cookies that we cut in half and used to make S'mores. They were way better than the traditional graham cracker version and inspired this recipe.

Yield: About 2 dozen

DIRECTIONS:

1. Preheat the oven to 350 degrees F. Line a baking sheet with parchment paper or a silicone baking mat.

2. Cream together the melted butter and brown sugar on medium-low speed. Add the egg yolks and mix until combined. Add the baking soda, salt, xanthan gum, and vanilla and mix until combined.

3. Add the flour, and mix until incorporated (first at low speed and then turn the speed up.) Then mix in the chocolate chips.

4. Scoop using a 1½ tablespoon cookie scoop and place cookies 4 inches apart on the prepared baking sheet.

5. Bake for 5 minutes and then gently press the marshmallows and chocolate bars into the top. Bake for another 5 minutes. The cookies should spread and will lose their doughy shine, but will still be very soft. Allow to cool on the baking sheet for a few minutes before moving to a cooling rack to finish cooling.

INGREDIENTS:

4 ounces (½ cup) butter, melted

5.5 ounces (½ cup + 3 tablespoons firmly packed) brown sugar

2 egg YOLKS

½ teaspoon xanthan gum

½ teaspoon baking soda

1 teaspoon vanilla

9 ounces (1½ cups plus 2 tablespoons cup) GF Cookie Blend

6 ounces (1 cup) chocolate chips

1.5 ounces (1 cup) mini marshmallows

1 chocolate bar, broken into pieces

Bacon Cookies

Bacon? In a cookie? These were definitely a favorite when I sold cookies at the local farmer's market. I think if I hadn't given out samples, many people wouldn't have ever tried them, but bacon in a sweet brown sugar cookie base is just a match made in heaven. Salty and sweet, like a chocolate covered pretzel or maple sausage. Just give them a chance.

Yield: About 2 dozen

Directions:

1. Preheat the oven to 350 degrees F. Line a baking sheet with parchment paper or a silicone baking mat.

2. Cream together the melted butter and brown sugar. Add the egg yolks and mix until combined. Add the baking soda, salt, xanthan gum, and vanilla, and mix until combined.

3. Add the flour, and mix until incorporated. Then mix in the chocolate chips (optional) and the crumbled bacon.

4. Scoop using a 1½ tablespoon cookie scoop and place cookies 4 inches apart on the prepared baking sheet.

5. Bake for approximately 10 minutes. The cookies should spread and will lose thier doughy shine, but will still be very soft. Allow to cool on the baking sheet for a few minutes before moving to a cooling rack to finish cooling.

Ingredients:

2 ounces (¼ cup) butter, melted

2 ounces (¼ cup) bacon fat (from bacon in recipe)

5.5 ounces (½ cup + 3 tablespoons firmly packed) brown sugar

2 egg YOLKS

½ teaspoon xanthan gum

½ teaspoon baking soda

1 teaspoon vanilla

9 ounces (1½ cups plus 2 tablespoons) GF Cookie Blend

½ pound bacon, cooked until crisp, and crumbled

(optional) 4.5 ounces (¾ cup) chocolate chips

Fluffernutter Cookies

If you've never had a fluffernutter cookie, you are in for a special treat. Something beautiful happens to peanut butter when you combine it with marshmallows; in a way it almost tastes more peanut-buttery once the richness is softened with some nice puffy mallows. Fluffernutter just may be my favorite variation on a peanut butter cookie.

Yield: About 16 cookies

DIRECTIONS:

1. Preheat oven to 350 degrees F. Line baking sheets with parchment paper or silicone baking mats.

2. Mix together the peanut butter, sugar, egg and salt until smooth.

3. Scoop using a 1½ tablespoon cookie scoop and place 2-3 inches apart on the lined baking sheets.

4. Flatten each cookie using the heel of your hand.

5. Bake for 5 minutes, press 4-5 marshmallows into the top of each cookie, and return to the oven for an additional 3-5 minutes.

6. Cool for a few minutes on the baking sheet before moving to a cooling rack to finish cooling.

INGREDIENTS:

1 cup peanut butter

6 ounces (¾ cup) white sugar

1 egg

¼ teaspoon salt

½ cup mini marshmallows

Double Fudge with Dried Cherries

Just as I was graduating from high school I made this recipe and shared it on my first blog, a blog that was mostly for sharing college papers. They aren't as dark chocolate as my Flourless Triple Chocolate, but are just as rich and gooey with melted chocolate. I love finding the sweet, slightly tart, dried cherries in the cookies. They keep the cookie from being too chocolatey (is there really such a thing?) by adding that little fruity bite. The cinnamon adds a depth of flavor and slight spiciness; you almost can't taste what it is, it is that little hint flavor on your tongue that you can't determine.

Yield: 2½-3 dozen

DIRECTIONS:

1. Preheat the oven to 350 degrees F. Line your baking sheets with parchment paper or a silicone baking mat.

2. In a double boiler (or a heat-proof bowl over a pan with a few inches of simmering water) melt the unsweetened and semisweet chocolate with the butter and then remove from heat. (alternatively microwave for 15 seconds, stir and repeat until melted.) Stir in the sugars and vanilla. Add the eggs and stir until thick and glossy (be careful that you stir as you add the eggs so that they don't scramble)

3. In another bowl whisk the GF Cookie Blend with the cocoa, cinnamon, and salt. Add these dry ingredients into the melted chocolate and stir until just combined. Add the chocolate chips and cherries.

4. Drop the batter onto the baking sheets using a 1½ tablespoon cookie scoop. Space the cookies about 3 inches apart.

5. Bake 10-12 minutes or until the cookies lose their shine around the edges. They should be set but still soft and fudgy.

INGREDIENTS:

2 ounces (¼ cup) butter

4 ounces (⅝ cup) chocolate, dark or semisweet

2.5 ounces (¼ cup +1 tablespoon firmly packed) brown sugar

6 ounces (¾ cup) white sugar

2 eggs

½ teaspoon cinnamon

¼ teaspoon salt

½ teaspoon vanilla

⅛ teaspoon xanthan gum

2.75 ounces (½ cup) flour GF Cookie Blend

1 ounces (¼ cup) cocoa powder

5 ounces (¾ cup) chocolate chips

2 ounces (¼ cup plus 2 tablespoons) dried cherries

Rocky Road Chocolate Cookies

Rocky Road is such a traditional flavor, I thought this book wouldn't be complete without my own Rocky Road Cookie, a rich chocolate cookie studded with nuts and chocolate chips. I add the marshmallows on the top instead of mixing them in because any that touch the pan, during baking, get too hot and melt into an unrecognizable gooey mess. When placed on top they stay perfectly puffy and toasty.

Yield: About 1½ dozen

DIRECTIONS:

1. Preheat your oven to 350 degrees F. Line your baking sheets with parchment paper or a silicone baking mat.

2. Cream together the butter and sugar. Add the egg and mix until combined. Add the vanilla, salt, baking soda, and cocoa powder and mix until you have a smooth dough. Reserve approximately ¼ cup of the chocolate chips and half of the nuts for pressing in the tops of the cookies. Stir in the rest of the chocolate chips and nuts until distributed throughout.

3. Scoop the dough using a 1½ tablespoon cookie scoop and drop 3 inches apart on your baking sheets. After 5 minutes press the marshmallows and nuts into the top of the cookies. Return to the oven and bake for another 5-7 minutes, approximately 10-12 minutes in all. They should lose their doughy shine on the top but will still be very soft.

4. Immediately after they come out of the oven press the reserved chocolate chips into the tops of the cookies.

5. Allow to cool on the baking sheet for several minutes to allow the cookies to firm up before moving to a cooling rack.

INGREDIENTS:

4 ounces (½ cup) butter, softened

4 ounces (1 cup) powdered sugar

1 egg

1 teaspoon vanilla

½ teaspoon baking soda

½ teaspoon salt

4 ounce(1 cup) cocoa powder

5.25 ounces (½ cup) milk, semisweet, or dark chocolate chips, divided

.75 ounces (½ cup) mini marshmallows

2 ounces (½ cup) chopped nuts (almonds, pecans, walnuts, or other nut of your choice.

Flourless Chocolate Hazelnut

....

I know that chocolate hazelnut spread (that happens to be gluten-free) is one of my favorites, and might be yours too. This cookie has all the same flavors; the sweet nutty hazelnuts and rich chocolate. I like the extra texture and crunch that granulated sugar gives this recipe. If you don't like it, just substitute powdered sugar.

Yield: About 1½ dozen

DIRECTIONS:

1. Preheat the oven to 350 degrees F. Line your baking sheets with parchment paper or a silicone baking mat.

2. Cream together the butter and sugar. Add the egg and mix until combined. Add the vanilla, salt, baking soda, ground hazelnuts, and cocoa powder and mix until you have a smooth dough. Stir in the chopped hazelnuts and the 3.5 ounces (½ cup) of the chocolate chips until distributed throughout.

3. Scoop the dough using a 1½ tablespoon cookie scoop and drop 3 inches apart on your baking sheets. Bake for approximately 10 minutes. They should lose their doughy shine on the top but will still be very soft.

4. Immediately after they come out of the oven press the rest of the chocolate chips (from the remaining amount) into the tops of the cookies.

5. Allow to cool on the baking sheet for several minutes to allow the cookies to firm up before moving to a cooling rack.

INGREDIENTS:

- 4 ounces (½ cup) butter, softened
- 4 ounces (½ cup) brown sugar
- 4 ounces (½ cup) white sugar
- 1 egg
- 1 teaspoon vanilla
- ½ teaspoon baking soda
- ½ teaspoon salt
- 4 ounce(1 cup) cocoa powder
- 1.25 ounces (¼ cup) ground hazelnuts
- 2½ ounces (½ cup) chopped hazelnuts
- 5.25 ounces (¾ cup) chocolate chips or chunks, divided

Cranberry White Chocolate Oatmeal

While I don't like raisins, I love dried cranberries, especially when they are in a white chocolate chip and oatmeal cookie. I love them so much, I once made cupcakes the mimicked the flavor of these cookies.

Yield: About 2 dozen

DIRECTIONS:

1. Preheat the oven to 350 degrees F. Line a baking sheet with parchment paper or a silicone baking mat.

2. In a stand mixer cream together the melted butter and brown sugar on medium-low speed. Add the eggs and mix until combined. Add the baking soda, salt, xanthan gum, honey, cinnamon, and vanilla and mix until combined.

3. Add the flour and oats and mix until incorporated. Then mix in the chocolate chips.

4. Scoop using a 1½ tablespoon cookie scoop and place cookies 2-3 inches apart on the prepared baking sheet.

5. Bake for 10 minutes. The cookies should spread and will lose their doughy shine, but will still be very soft. Allow to cool on the baking sheet for a few minutes before moving to a cooling rack to finish cooling.

INGREDIENTS:

4 ounces (½ cup) butter, melted

5.5 ounces (¾ cup + 2 tablespoons firmly packed) brown sugar

2 egg YOLKS

½ teaspoon xanthan gum

½ teaspoon salt

½ teaspoon baking soda

1 teaspoon vanilla

½ teaspoon cinnamon

1 tablespoon honey

11 ounces (2 cups) GF Cookie Blend

3 ounces (¾ cup) rolled GF oats

6 ounces (1 cup) white chocolate chips

2½ ounces (½ cup) craisins

Cake Batter Cookies

Cake batter has been another trend that has taken over Pinterest. I loved the idea and was excited to capture all the sweet buttery flavors of cake batter in a cookie; complete with sprinkles.

Yield: 1½ dozen

Directions:

1. Preheat the oven to 350 degrees F. Line your baking sheets with parchment paper or silicone baking mats.

2. In a stand mixer or mixing bowl, mix together the melted butter and sugar on medium-low speed. Add the egg and mix until combined. Add the salt, baking powder, baking soda, xanthan gum, and mix until combined.

3. Add the GF Cookie Blend and mix until incorporated. Add the white chocolate chips and sprinkles and mix just until they are evenly distributed throughout.

4. Scoop the cookies using a 1½ tablespoon cookie scoop and place the dough 2-3 inches apart on the prepared baking sheet. Bake for 10 minutes or until the cookies lose their doughy shine and have spread slightly.

5. If desired, flatten the cookies slightly by pressing down on them slightly with a spatula. This will give them a nice crinkle on the top and keep them from looking too puffy. (Entirely optional, it won't affect the taste.) If desired, press additional white chocolate chips into the tops of the cookies.

Ingredients:

- 2 ounces (¼ cup) butter, melted
- 4 ounces (½ cup) white sugar
- 1 egg
- ½ teaspoon salt
- ½ teaspoon baking powder
- ¼ teaspoon baking soda
- ½ teaspoon xanthan gum
- ¾ teaspoon vanilla
- 6.5 ounces (1¼ cups) GF Cookie Blend
- 3 ounces (½ cup) white chocolate chips +additional for putting in the top (optional)
- 2 tablespoons sprinkles

Chocolate Puddle Cookies

Cookies exchanges are no easy thing for people like us. What do you do if you, or anyone else in the exchange, has a dietary restriction? You try to find recipes that will work for everyone, that's what. Here are two no-flour, easy-to-bake cookie recipes. You can serve these to a mixed crowd and no one will even know they are gluten-free.

Directions:

1. Preheat oven to 320 degrees F. and position racks in the top and bottom third. Line three (preferably rimmed) baking sheets with parchment paper or silicone baking mats. Or you can bake in batches with fewer pans.

2. Make sure your walnuts have cooled a bit, then chop coarsely and set aside. Sift together the confectioner's sugar, cocoa powder, and sea salt. Stir in the walnuts, then add the egg whites and vanilla. Stir until well combined.

3. Spoon the batter onto the prepared sheets in mounds of about 2 tablespoons each, allowing for PLENTY of room between cookies. These cookies are like reverse Shrinky Dinks—they really expand. Don't try to get more than 6 cookies on each sheet, and try to avoid placing the batter too close to the edge of the pan.

4. Bake until they puff up. The tops should get glossy and then crack a bit after 12 -15 minutes. Have faith, they look sad at first, then really blossom. You may want to rotate the pans in the oven as they cook.

5. Slide the cookies still on parchment onto a cooling rack, and let them cool completely. They will keep in an airtight for a couple days.

Triumph Dining Blog

Ingredients:

10.9 ounces walnut halves (toasted and cooled)

16 ounces (4 cup) powdered sugar

2 ounces (½ cup) unsweetened cocoa powder

½ teaspoon salt (fine grain sea salt)

4 large egg whites (room temperature)

1 tablespoon vanilla

5 Ingredient Chocolate Chip Cookies

Yield: About a dozen small cookies

Directions:

1. Preheat oven to 350 degrees F. Line baking sheets with parchment paper or silicone baking mats.

2. Mix all ingredients except chocolate chips.

3. When blended, mix in the chocolate chips.

4. Using your fingers, form 1½ inch balls (dough will be very wet and sticky) and place onto an un-greased parchment lined cookie sheet. You don't want to make them too big because they do spread.

5. Bake for 9 minutes. Let the cookies sit on the cookies sheet for about 30 seconds to 1 minute before letting cool on a wire rack.

Triumph Dining Blog

Ingredients:

1 cup creamy peanut butter

8 ounces (1 cup) firmly packed brown sugar

1 large egg

1 teaspoon baking soda

4 ounces (½ cup) milk chocolate chips

Double Chocolate Chunk Cookies

These gluten free double chocolate chunk cookies are truly out of this world. I hope you get to try them soon. You will not be disappointed.

Directions:

1. Preheat oven to 350 degrees F. Line two cookie sheets with parchment paper or silicone baking mats and set aside.

2. In a microwave-safe dish, melt 5 ounces of the chocolate chunks in 45-second intervals, stirring the chocolate in between. Set aside.

3. In a large mixing bowl, with a wire whisk, (you can also use a stand mixer), add the eggs, sugar, and oil and beat until combine. Add the vanilla and melted chocolate and beat constantly while you add it.

4. Add the flour, baking soda, salt, cocoa powder, and the remaining chocolate chunks (if using, add the chili powder as well) and combine. I do this step with a rubber spatula.

5. With a medium cookie scoop, scoop cookie batter on each baking sheet about 2 inches apart. Bake for 10-12 minutes. Cool cookies on a wire rack and store in an airtight container.

Miryam Doblas, Eat Good 4 Life

Ingredients:

2 eggs

½ cup olive oil

1 teaspoon vanilla

6 ounces (¾ cup) unrefined sugar

8.25 ounces (1½) cup brown rice flour

2 ounces (½ cup) cocoa powder

1 teaspoon aluminum free baking soda

10 ounces dark chocolate chunks

1 teaspoon chili Ancho powder, optional

Pinch of salt

Oatmeal Peanut Butter Cookies

These simple peanut butter cookies are crispy on the outside, but melt in your mouth as you eat them. The cookie jar never stays full when these are around!

DIRECTIONS:

1. Preheat oven to 350 degrees F. Line two cookie sheets with parchment paper or silicone baking mats and set aside.

2. Cream peanut butter, coconut oil and brown sugar.

3. Add egg and vanilla.

4. Combine GF Cookie Blend, oatmeal, baking soda, salt, and cinnamon in a small bowl.

5. Mix dry ingredients into peanut butter mixture.

6. Drop dough by teaspoonfuls onto a baking sheet.

7. Press down with a fork or flat bottom of a glass.

8. Bake for 12 minutes or until cookies begin to brown around the edges.

Kristen Baker, Frugal Antics of a Harried Homemaker

INGREDIENTS:

½ cup creamy natural peanut butter

½ cup coconut oil

8 ounces (1 cup) brown sugar, firmly packed

1 egg

1 teaspoon vanilla

5.5 ounces (1 cup) GF Cookie Blend

2 ounces (½ cup) gluten free rolled oats

1 teaspoon baking soda

½ teaspoon salt

1 teaspoon cinnamon

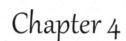

Chapter 4

Rolled, Sliced, and Other Stuff

Flourless Peanut Butter & Jam Thumbprints

Peanut butter and jelly make the iconic sandwich and I couldn't resist using the same well loved flavor combination in these cookies. Rich peanut butter and fruity jam pair perfectly. Raspberry is always my favorite, but try any jam flavor you like

Yield: 16 cookies

DIRECTIONS:

1. Preheat oven to 350 degrees F. Line baking sheets with parchment paper or silicone baking mats.

2. Mix together the peanut butter, sugar, egg, and salt until smooth.

3. Scoop using a 1½ tablespoon cookie scoop and place 2-3 inches apart on the lined baking sheets.

4. Use your thumb, or the wrong end of a wooden spoon, to make an impression in the middle of each cookie. Spoon a teaspoon of jam or jelly into each impression.

5. Bake for 8-10 minutes. Cool for a few minutes on the baking sheet before moving to a cooling rack to finish cooling.

INGREDIENTS:

1 cup peanut butter

6 ounces (¾ cup) white sugar

1 egg

¼ teaspoon salt (omit if using salted peanut butter)

¼ cup of your favorite jam or jelly

Peppermint Sugar Cookies

These are my favorite sugar cookies to make at Christmastime. Everything you love about your favorite soft frosted sugar cookies, but with just a hint of festive peppermint. They taste so light, I have to be careful no to eat too many.

Yield: 2½-3 dozen

Directions:

1. Add ¼ teaspoon of peppermint to the pre-made *American Buttercream* frosting. Taste the frosting and add more peppermint if the flavor isn't strong enough. Peppermints often vary in concentration, but are often very strong. Load the frosting into a piping bag fitted with a large round tip.

2. Frost each cookie, starting in the middle and swirling outward so that the whole cookie is covered in an even layer of frosting. If desired, smooth the frosting with a baby bent spatula or a butter knife.

3. Sprinkle with the crushed candy canes. Store in an airtight container at room temperature for 2-3 days or freeze up to 2 months.

Ingredients:

1 recipe sugar cookie dough, rolled, cut, and baked.

1 recipe *American Buttercream*, vanilla omitted

¼-½ teaspoon peppermint

3-4 chocolate covered candy canes, crushed (or regular candy canes)

Frosting

3x batch of *American Buttercream*, page 139

Chia Shortbread

· ·

Don't skip the chia in these shortbread! The chia seeds add a lot of structure to the shortbread, making the dough and finished cookies much easier to handle and keeps them from falling apart. The chia also adds a subtle nuttiness to the cookies. If you don't like chia, or don't have it on hand, this recipe just won't turn out. This shortbread isn't the more traditional super buttery and rich shortbread, instead it is light and crisp. The perfect cookie to have with a cup of tea or glass of cider.

Yield: 24 sticks

DIRECTIONS:

1. Preheat the oven to 350 degrees F. Line a baking sheet with parchment paper or a silicone baking mat.

2. Cream together the butter and sugar. Add the flour, chia seeds mixed with water, and salt and mix until a smooth dough forms.

3. Place dough directly onto a baking sheet lined with parchment or a silcone baking mat and roll out until it is rectangle in shape and ¼ inch thick.

4. Score into sticks that are approximately 1" x 3 ½" and bake in the preheated oven for 20-25 minutes. The shortbread may still be a little soft when it is done but will lose its doughy shine (it will crisp up as it cools.)

5. Cool, dust with powdered sugar, and break apart.

INGREDIENTS:

4 ounces (½ cup) butter, softened

11 ounces (2 cups) GF Cookie Blend

2 ounces (½ cup) powdered sugar

¼ teaspoon salt

2 tablespoons ground chia seeds mixed with ¼ cup water

Chewy Coconut Caramel Cookies

Oh how I loved girl scout cookies back in my gluten-eating days! The cookie that I missed the absolute most were those little rings that were covered in toasted coconut and sweet caramel and then dipped and drizzled in chocolate. Here is my gluten-free version of those favorites. I've even found a few shortcuts to make the chocolate coating process super easy.

Yield: 1½ dozen cookies

DIRECTIONS:

1. Cream the butter and sugar together. Add the eggs and beat until combined.

2. Add the salt, baking powder, xanthan gum, and vanilla Then add the GF Cookie Blend and mix until combined.

3. Chill the dough for at least 1 hour.

4. Preheat the oven to 350 F. Line your baking sheets with parchment paper or silicone baking mats.

5. Roll out the dough between 2 sheets of plastic wrap. Cut into 2½ inch circles, and cut a small round hole out of the middle of each circle, about 1 inch across. Move to the baking sheets, placed at least 2 inches apart.

6. Bake for about 10 minutes, the cookies will lose their doughy shine and will be set, but will still be very soft.

7. Cool for a few minutes on the baking sheets before moving to a cooling rack to cool completely.

8. To make the coconut caramel topping, melt the sugar in a heavy bottomed saucepan over medium heat. Pour the sugar in the pan and watch for the edges to start to melt. Once they do, stir the sugar until it is all liquid and has a nice caramel color (a few clump may form, but don't worry about them too much. You can strain them out later and you don't want to cook the sugar too far and have it burn.)

9. Turn the heat down to medium-low and add the cream and vanilla, stir until it all melts back together. When you first add the cream, the sugar will harden, but it will melt into the cream within a few minutes; just be patient and continue to stir while the mixture bubbles.

(continued on next page)

Ingredients:

4 ounces (½ cup) butter, softened

4 ounces (½ cup) sugar

1 egg

½ teaspoon salt

¾ teaspoon baking powder

¾ teaspoon xanthan gum

¾ teaspoon vanilla

9 ounces (1½ cups) GF Cookie Blend

Coconut Caramel Topping:

12 ounces (1½ cup) sugar

1 cup heavy or whipping cream

2 ounces (¼ cup) butter

1 teaspoon vanilla

¼ teaspoon salt

7.25 ounces (2 ¼ cup) coconut, toasted

8 ounces chocolate coating (like almond bark)

10. Once you have a smooth mixture (with maybe a few hard to melt clumps) add the butter, 1 tablespoon at a time, and swirl it around the pan until it melts. Add the salt and then pour the caramel through a sieve to remove any hard sugar clumps.

11. Mix with the toasted coconut.

To put it all together, frost the cookies with the coconut caramel mixture.

1. Melt the chocolate coating according to the directions on it's package. Pour the chocolate coating into a sandwich sized plastic bag, twist the top or seal the bag so that the chocolate doesn't escape and then cut a small corner off of the bag.

2. On a piece of parchment or clean silicone baking mat pipe a ring about the same size as the cookie and then press the cookie on top of it. This will easily coat the bottom of the cookies in chocolate without having to dip it. The cookie looks a lot more neat and the process is much cleaner and easier than dipping. Repeat with the remaining cookies.

3. Drizzle the tops of all the cookies with some chocolate, going back and forth in one direction. Allow the chocolate to set.

Chocolate Chip Cheese Loaf

Serve with Aunt Joanne's Fire Cookies on the next page.

DIRECTIONS:

1. Mix together the cream cheese, powdered sugar, and cinnamon.

2. Using plastic wrap, form the mixture into a log or ball

3. Chill for at least half an hour and then roll in the mini chocolate chips. Re-wrap in fresh plastic wrap and chill for 1-2 hours, or until serving time. It also freezes well, up to 2 months. Just thaw before serving.

INGREDIENTS:

8 ounces cream cheese, softened

1.3 ounces (⅓ cup) powdered sugar

1 teaspoon ground cinnamon

½ cup mini chocolate chips

Aunt Joanne's Fire Cookies

The legend to these cookies is that Aunt Joanne's mom was making her favorite gingersnaps one day and instead of a teaspoon of ginger, put in a whole TABLESPOON by mistake. Those cookies were spicy, but Aunt Joanne and her siblings loved them so much that from then on their mom always used the extra ginger. My favorite way to fight the heat is with my Cinnamon Chocolate Cream Cheese Loaf (page 73), but a tall glass of cold milk works well too. I've also made these cookies egg and dairy free, so that everyone can enjoy them.

Yield: 1½ dozen

DIRECTIONS:

1. Preheat oven to 350 degrees F. Line baking sheets with parchment paper or silicone baking mat.

2. In a stand mixer, cream together the sugar and shortening. Add chia seeds mixed with water and molasses and mix until smooth. Add all the remaining ingredients and mix on low speed until things start to incorporate, and then mix on medium speed until a smooth dough is formed.

3. Scoop using a 1½ tablespoon cookie scoop and roll into a ball. Roll in sugar and place at least 3 inches apart on the baking sheet. Bake for 12-14 minutes. Cool for a few minutes on the baking sheet before moving to a cooling rack to finish cooling.

4. Serve with Chocolate Chip Cheese Loaf (page 73).

INGREDIENTS:

2.75 ounces (¼ cup plus 2 tablespoons) vegetable shortening

2.6 ounces (⅓ cup) white sugar

1½ ounces (2 tablespoons) molasses

½ tablespoon ground chia seeds mixed with 1 tablespoon water

2.5 teaspoon ground ginger

1 teaspoon baking soda

½ teaspoon cinnamon

¼ teaspoon salt

5.5 ounces (1 cup) GF Cookie Blend

approximately 8 ounces (1 cup) white sugar (for rolling)

Chocolate Crinkles

I just love watching these cookies bake because the buttery chocolate dough spreads to leave the little crinkles everywhere. Sweet powdered sugar on the outside and rich chocolate on the inside; these cookies are tons of fun.

Yield: About 2 dozen

DIRECTIONS:

1. Preheat the oven to 350 degrees F. Line your baking sheets with parchment paper or silicone baking mats.

2. In a medium mixing bowl mix together the sugar and oil. Add the eggs and stir until combined. Add all the remaining ingredients, except the powdered sugar, and stir until combined. You will have a thick, but still soft dough.

3. Put the powdered sugar into a small bowl. Scoop the batter using a 1½ tablespoon cookie scoop and drop it into the powdered sugar. Roll the dough to coat and place it on the baking sheet. Repeat with the rest of the dough, placing the cookies 3-4 inches apart.

4. Bake for 8-10 minutes. The cookies will spread and crack slightly, and lose some of their shine. The cookies will still be soft and will set up more as they cool.

INGREDIENTS:

1½ ounces (½ cup) cocoa

6.25 ounces (¾ cup) sugar

¼ cup oil

2 eggs

5.5 ounces (1 cup) GF Cookie Blend

1 teaspoon vanilla

1 teaspoon baking powder

¼ teaspoon salt

approximately ½ cup powdered sugar

White Chocolate Cherry Kaleidoscope Cookies

The bright colors of these cookies remind me of a kaleidoscope, especially because of the way the cookies are sliced so the bright color of the candied cherries really shines. These are great for making ahead and storing the dough in the freezer; whenever you need cookies just slice and bake.

Yield: 3-4 dozen

DIRECTIONS:

1. Cream together the butter and sugar until fluffy.

2. Add the eggs and mix until combined.

3. Add the salt, baking powder, and xanthan gum and mix until just combined. Add the GF Cookie Blend, ½ cup at a time until it has all been incorporated.

4. Add the white chocolate chips and candied cherries and mix until evenly distributed throughout.

5. Lay out a piece of plastic wrap on a flat working surface and place half of the dough on it. Form the dough into a log, wrap in the plastic wrap, and freeze until firm.

6. Repeat with the other half of dough.

7. Preheat your oven to 350 degrees F.

8. Slice the chilled dough into ¼ inch slices and place on a baking sheet.

9. Bake for 8-10 minutes, or until the bottom just barely starts to turn golden.

The cookie will still be white and will be a bit soft, but will set up as it cools.

INGREDIENTS:

4 ounces (½ cup) butter, softened

8 ounces (1 cup) white sugar

2 eggs

¾ teaspoon salt

1½ teaspoon baking powder

1½ teaspoon xanthan gum

16.5 ounces GF Cookie Blend

1 cup white chocolate chips

1 cup chopped candied cherries

Biscochitos

· ·

If you don't live in New Mexico chances are that you may have never even heard of Biscochitos. They are a sweet and fragrant roll out cookie flavored with cinnamon and freshly ground anise. This recipe doesn't have as much anise as some recipes, which keeps the flavor subtle instead of overpowering. Also, you might think it odd to use lard in a cookie, and normally it would be. The lard makes the cookie light and flaky (almost like a good pie crust) . Before this recipe I thought I wouldn't like biscochitos (licorice flavored cardboard was what I had imagined) but if you make them right, they just melt in your mouth. (Don't be tempted to taste the dough though, it isn't good until after you bake them.)

Yield: About 3-4 dozen

DIRECTIONS:

1. Cream the lard with sugar and freshly ground anise seeds until *very* fluffy in a stand mixer, or using electric beaters (about 5 minutes)

2. Beat in the egg.

3. Add the xanthan gum, salt, baking powder, GF Cookie Blend, and cider and mix until well blended.

4. Cover with plastic wrap and refrigerate 1-2 hours. (Cover with plastic wrap so the dough doesn't dry out.)

5. Divide the dough into 3-4 more manageable portions and roll it out between 2 pieces of plastic wrap until it is ¼ inch thick.

6. Cut into shapes with cookie cutter (about 2-2½ inches across) .

7. Mix the ¾ cup sugar and 2 tablespoons of cinnamon in a small bowl.

8. Dip tops of the cut out cookies in the cinnamon-sugar mixture.

9. Bake 10-12 minutes or until edges start to turn a golden color.

10. Remove from oven and immediately dip the cookies in the cinnamon-sugar mixture again.

11. Place cookies on cooling sheet and allow to cool completely.

Recipe adapted from Renee Quintana of Tortillas and Honey

INGREDIENTS:

16.5 ounces (3 cup) GF Cookie Blend

¾ teaspoon xanthan gum

¼ teaspoon salt

1½ teaspoon baking powder

6 ounces (¾ cup) white sugar

1½ teaspoon anise seed, freshly ground or smashed

1 egg

8 ounces (1 cup) lard

2 tablespoons apple cider

Topping:

¾ cup sugar

2 tablespoons cinnamon

Funfetti Cookies

These cookies are just fun! Traditional sugar cookies swirled with color and rolled in sprinkles, they are perfect for any holiday. I made a bunch of big pink ones for a Valentine's day dance, and even more mini ones that we put in little cellophane bags to hand out at a church Halloween party. You can do any color combination, the possibilities are endless.

Yield: 2-2½ dozen ½" thick cookies or 4-5 dozen ¼" cookies.

DIRECTIONS:

1. In the bowl of your stand mixer cream the butter and sugar together on low-medium speed. Add the eggs and beat until combined.

2. Add the salt, baking powder, xanthan gum, and vanilla. Then add the GF Cookie Blend and mix until combined.

3. Divide the dough in half and color half with food coloring, in the color of your choice.

4. Between 2 sheets of plastic wrap roll out the uncolored portion of the dough so that it is a rectangle approximately 10" x 12" and is ¼ inch thick. Set aside and roll the colored dough out between 2 sheets of plastic wrap so that it is approximately the same size and thickness of the uncolored dough. Place the colored dough directly on top of the uncolored dough, with the long edge closest to you body. Carefully roll the dough away from you so that you have a nice log. Roll the log in sprinkles to coat what will become the outside edges of the cookies. Wrap the log of dough in plastic wrap and freeze until firm (or until you are ready to bake.)

5. When you are ready to bake the cookies preheat the oven to 350 degrees F. Line a baking sheet with parchment or a silicone baking mat.

6. Remove the dough from the freezer and slice into ½ inch thick slices (turn the log ¼ turn each time you slice to prevent getting a flat edge). Place the rounds on the cookie sheet, 2 inches apart.

7. Bake for 12-14 minutes or until the cookies lose their doughy shine and are slightly set (they will still be super soft if you touch them.) Be careful not to leave them in too long because you want to avoid golden edges if possible. Allow to cool for several minutes on the sheet before moving to a cooling rack to finish cooling. (Alternatively slice into ¼ inch thick slices and bake for 8-10 minutes.)

INGREDIENTS:

6 ounces (¾ cup) butter, softened

12 ounces (1½ cup) sugar

3 eggs

1 teaspoon salt

2¼ teaspoon baking powder

2¼ teaspoon xanthan gum

2¼ teaspoon vanilla

27 ounces (4¾ cups + 1 tablespoon) GF Cookie Blend

Gel food coloring

Sprinkles

German Chocolate

Bittersweet brownie cookies topped with the traditional coconut pecan frosting. It is used as frosting, and everyone calls it frosting, but it is really more like a custard. Don't be scared of making a stove-top frosting. Basically you just whisk everything together and heat it up, really easy and the results are delicious.

Yield: About 2 dozen

DIRECTIONS:

1. Preheat the oven to 350 degrees F. Line a baking sheet with parchment paper or a silicone baking mat.

2. In a stand mixer cream together the butter and sugar on medium-low speed. Add the eggs and mix until combined. Add the cocoa, baking powder, salt, and xanthan gum, and mix until combined.

3. Add the flour, and mix until incorporated.

4. Scoop using a 1½ tablespoon cookie scoop and place cookies 3 inches apart on the prepared baking sheet. Flatten slightly with the heel of your hand.

5. Bake for 8-10 minutes until the cookies lose their doughy shine. The cookies will still be soft. Let them cool for a few minutes on the sheet before moving to a cooling rack to finish cooling. Once cooled completely frost with the coconut pecan frosting.

INGREDIENTS:

3 ounces (6 tablespoons) butter, softened

9 ounces (1 cup plus 2 tablespoons) sugar

3 eggs

3 ounces (¾ cup) cocoa

6 ounces (1 cup plus 2 tablespoons) GF Cookie Blend

1½ teaspoon baking powder

¾ teaspoon salt

½ teaspoon xanthan gum

German Cholate Frosting, page 143

Fortune Cookies

You can finally have your fortune and eat it too! I think that these cookies taste even better than their take-out counterparts and you can put whatever fortunes you like inside. Making cookies on a griddle may take some getting used to, but for these cookies it is much easier than using an oven. You might burn the tips of your fingers working with these hot cookies, but the results are well worth it.

They are best if eaten the day you make them or the next. They will soften and get a little chewy if you save them longer. If you don't eat them in time just crisp them up again in the oven and they will be nice and fresh.

Yield: About 1 dozen fortune-filled cookies

DIRECTIONS:

1. Cut strips of paper (or wax paper) that are approximately ½" x 2½" and write your desired fortunes on them.

2. Whip the egg whites until foamy, but not until peaks form.

3. Sift in the dry ingredients and add all the other ingredients, and beat to combine. The batter will be very thin, thinner than pancake batter.

4. Heat a nonstick skillet or griddle until a drop of water sizzles and dances across the surface (about 350 degrees F.) Drop 1 tablespoon of batter onto the hot griddle. Immediately spread it around using the back side of the spoon so that it is approximately 3 inches in diameter, working quickly to not leave trails in partially cooked batter (those trails or thinner spots will cause the cookie to cook unevenly and burn in areas.) You will have to spread the batter pretty thin, but that is OK.

5. Once the top starts to look dry and the edges are a little brown (anywhere from 3-5 minutes if your pan is hot) use a rubber spatula to turn the cookie. If the cookie doesn't come up easily let it cook for another 30 seconds and try again. Cook for an additional 2-3 minutes on the second side, until it is lightly browned. Immediately after removing it from the skillet, place the fortune in the center of the cookie, fold the cookie in half, touching the top edges together, place the cookie on the rim of the bowl with top edges towards the ceiling and bend the cookie by pulling the sides toward the counter top. Place the cookie in a muffin pan to help it keep its shape. Repeat with the remaining batter.

6. Preheat the oven to 250 degrees F. and bake the cookies in the muffin tin to crisp them up, for an additional 20 minutes (optional, but it will help the cookies to be more like the ones you get with your take-out.) Let cool completely. Only once they are cool completely will they be crisp.

INGREDIENTS:

2 egg whites

1.4 ounces (¼ cup) GF Cookie Blend

2 ounces (¼ cup) white sugar

½ teaspoon almond extract

½ teaspoon vanilla

2 tablespoons oil, plus more for greasing the pan

¼ teaspoon salt

Almond Chocolate Biscotti

This biscotti was a huge hit with all of our families on New Years Eve. The entire batch was gone in a matter of minutes. These biscotti are crispy and crunchy; the flavors are simple and not over-powering and you can easily substitute your favorite nut if you don't like almonds. I love using mini chocolate chips because then every bite is sure to have lots of chocolate. If you don't have mini chips you can use normal chips, either as is or you can chop them smaller.

Yield: About 1½ dozen cookies

DIRECTIONS:

1. Preheat oven to 350 degrees F. Line a baking sheet with parchment paper or a silicone baking mat.

2. Cream butter and sugar, add eggs. Add GF Cookie Blend, xanthan gum, baking powder, almond meal and mix until smooth. Stir in almond extract and mini chocolate chips

3. Form into 2 loaves, approximately 10" x 6" each, directly on the prepared baking sheet (the dough will be sticky and is much easier to handle if you wet your hands with a little water before forming the dough.) Brush both loaves with milk using a pastry brush and bake for 30 minutes, let cool for at least 20-30 minutes, and slice into ½ inch diagonal slices. Bake for an additional 5-8 minutes on each side.

INGREDIENTS:

13.75 ounces (2½ cups) GF Cookie Blend

4 ounces (½ cup) butter, softened

8 ounces (1 cup) sugar

3 eggs

1½ teaspoon baking powder

1.75 ounces (½ cup) almond meal (or ground almonds)

1 teaspoon xanthan gum

½ cup mini chocolate chips

½ teaspoon almond extract

1-2 tablespoons milk

Lebkuchen

These are my mom's favorite cookie and she requests them every year at Christmas. Spicy gingerbread, traditionally they are glazed, but instead we dip them in chocolate. So soft and chewy, with that shiny chocolate shell, these cookies bring so many yummy flavors together.

Yield: About 3 dozen

DIRECTIONS:

1. Preheat oven to 350 degrees F. Line a baking sheet with parchment paper or a silicone baking mat.

2. Cream butter and sugar. Beat in the egg, molasses, and honey. Add the flour blend, spices, xanthan gum, baking powder, and salt. The dough will be like a stiff paste or very soft dough. Continue to mix or knead it by hand until smooth.

3. Chill at least an hour. Using a 1½ tablespoon cookie scoop, place on the baking sheet. Bake for 8-10 minutes.

4. Once cooled you can dip or decorate with melted chocolate as desired.

INGREDIENTS:

4 ounces butter (½ cup)

4 ounces (¾ cup) brown sugar

1 egg

¾ cup molasses

¼ cup honey

22 ounces (4 cups) GF Cookie Blend

1 teaspoon ginger

½ teaspoon cloves

¼ teaspoon chili powder

¾ teaspoon xanthan gum

2 teaspoon baking powder

1 teaspoon salt

Melted chocolate for dipping (optional)

Snowball Cookies

Snowball Cookies, or Mexican Wedding Cookies, or Russian Tea Cakes, whatever you call them, are another childhood favorite of mine. I remember making these at Christmas time with my mom when I was a little girl. My favorite part was rolling the cookies in the powdered sugar when they came out of the oven. We called them Snowball Cookies because that is what my mom had called them growing up, so that is what I still call them today.

Yield: About 3 dozen

DIRECTIONS:

1. Cream together the butter and sugar on medium-low speed. Add the salt, xanthan gum, and mix until combined.

2. Add the chopped nuts and GF Cookie Blend and mix until incorporated.

3. Chill the dough for 1 hour.

4. Preheat the oven to 350 degrees F. Line your baking sheets with silicone baking mats or parchment paper.

5. Scoop the cookies using a 1½ tablespoon cookie scoop and roll into balls. Place the dough balls 2 inches apart on the baking sheets. Bake for 10 minutes or until the cookies lose their doughy shine and the edges just start to turn golden.

6. While still hot, roll the cookies in powdered sugar to coat. Allow to cool before storing.

INGREDIENTS:

8 ounces (1 cup) butter, softened

3 ounces (¾ cup) powdered sugar

½ teaspoon salt

1 teaspoon vanilla

½ teaspoon xanthan gum

4 ounces (approximately ¾ cup) chopped nuts (pecans, walnuts, almonds, or your favorite)

11 ounces (2 cups) GF Cookie Blend

8 ounces (1 cup) powdered sugar, for coating the finished cookies.

Chapter 5

Sandwich Cookies

Oatmeal Creme Pies

I'm sure you recognize these iconic chewy oatmeal and molasses cookies filled with a sweet, white, fluffy cream, Marshmallow Fluff (see Chapter 7) . The secret to these cookies is to not use regular rolled oats without first pulsing them a few times in the food processor. This does wonders for the finished cookie, making it that soft and chewy sandwich that we all know and love.

Yield: 12 sandwiches

DIRECTIONS:

1. First put the oats in a food processor or blender and pulse several times until they are coarsely ground (you still want some larger pieces for texture so be careful to not over process it. Alternatively you could use quick oats.)

2. Mix together the melted butter and sugar. Add the egg yolk and mix until combined.

3. Add the xanthan gum, baking soda, cinnamon, vanilla, salt, and molasses. Mix to combine.

4. Add the oats and flour; mix to combine.

5. Scoop the dough using a 1½ tablespoon cookie scoop onto a baking sheet lined with a silicone baking mat or parchment paper, 6 per sheet. Leave at least 3-4 inches between the cookies to give them plenty of room to spread, they will.

6. Bake 8-10 minutes. The cookies will spread but will still be soft when you take them out. Allow them to cool for several minutes before removing them from the baking sheet to a cooling rack.

7. Spoon 1½–3 tablespoons of the Marshmallow Fluff filling onto a cookie and top with another cookie, pressing it down to spread the filling out to the edges.

INGREDIENTS:

4 ounces (½ cup) butter, melted

5.5 ounces (½ cup + 3 tablespoons firmly packed) brown sugar

2 egg yolks

½ teaspoon xanthan gum

½ teaspoon salt

1 teaspoon baking soda

1 teaspoon vanilla

1 teaspoon cinnamon

½ cup molasses

8 ounces (2 cups) rolled oats (or quick oats)

4 ounces (½ cup) GF Cookie Blend

FILLING:

Marshmallow Fluff, page 141

Red Velvet Cream Cheese Sandwiches

I absolutely love these soft and chewy sandwich cookies. Put cream cheese frosting on anything and I'll love it, but red velvet is just something special. Red velvet is basically a chocolate kissed vanilla cake that is a deep red in color. Traditionally part of the color comes from the reaction between baking soda, vinegar, and the cocoa powder, but I didn't use vinegar in these cookies because the extra moisture would have changed the texture of the cookies.

Yield: 12 sandwiches

DIRECTIONS:

1. Preheat the oven to 350 degrees F. Line a baking sheet with parchment paper or a silicone baking mat.

2. Cream together the melted butter and brown sugar. Add the eggs and mix until combined. Add the baking soda, salt, xanthan gum, and vanilla and mix until combined.

3. Add the cocoa, food coloring, and GF Cookie Blend, and mix until incorporated.

4. Scoop using 1½ tablespoon cookie scoop and place cookies 4 inches apart on the prepared baking sheet. (5 or 6 to a sheet.)

5. Bake for 8 minutes. The cookies will spread and will lose their doughy shine, but will still be very soft. Allow to cool on the baking sheet for a few minutes before moving to a cooling rack to finish cooling.

6. Cool completely before filling with Cream Cheese Frosting

INGREDIENTS:

4 ounces (½ cup) butter, melted

5.5 ounces (½ cup + 3 tablespoons firmly packed) brown sugar

2 eggs

½ teaspoon xanthan gum

½ teaspoon salt

½ teaspoon baking soda

1 teaspoon vanilla

½ ounces (2 tablespoons) cocoa powder

9 ounces (1½ cups + 1 tablespoon) GF Cookie Blend

1 teaspoon liquid red food coloring (or more or less as desired)

FILLING:

Cream Cheese Frosting, page 142

Crunchy Chocolate Sandwiches with Vanilla Crème

This recipe was one of the hardest to perfect. But it was well worth the time. I know that there are several gluten-free brands you can buy at the store, but sometimes you just want to make your own; it is a lot cheaper too. If you have a bad feelings toward shortening feel free to use another frosting to fill or use butter instead of the shortening. Just be warned that if you do make any filling substitutes, it won't taste the same as that iconic milk dunking cookie, but it will still be delicious.

Yield: 1½ dozen sandwiches

DIRECTIONS:

1. Preheat oven to 325 degrees F. Line baking sheets with parchment paper or silicone baking mat.

2. Cream together the butter and sugar. Add the egg and mix until combined.

3. Add the xanthan gum, cocoa powder, and salt and mix until combined.

4. Add the GF Cookie Blend and mix until the dough comes together. Depending on the humidity levels you may need to add a little water to bring the dough together and make it easier to work with. Add up to 1 tablespoon, a teaspoon at a time until the dough comes together.

5. Divide the dough in half and roll the first half of the dough out between 2 sheets of plastic wrap until it is ¼ inch thick. Cut out with 2 inch round cookie cutters and place half and inch apart on the prepared baking sheets and bake for 16-18 minutes. The cookie will be done when it loses its doughy shine and it will become firm. It will become more crisp as it cools.

6. Cool for a few minutes on the baking sheet before moving to a cooling rack. Allow to cool completely before filling with the creme filling.

7. To fill load the frosting into a piping bag or a plastic bag with the tip snipped off and pipe a circle of frosting in the center of the bottom of one cookie. Place another cookie on top and squeeze slightly to press the filling out to the edges.

INGREDIENTS:

COOKIE:

3 ounces (¼ cup plus 2 tablespoon) white sugar

2 ounces (¼ cup) butter, softened

1 egg

3 ounces (¾ cup) cocoa powder

¼ teaspoon xanthan gum

⅛ teaspoon salt

2.75 ounces (½ cup) GF Cookie Blend

1 tablespoon water (if necessary)

FILLING:

Vanilla Crème Filling, page 146

Raspberry Almond Linzer Cookies

I love the flavors of raspberry and almond in these pretty little cookies. The little hint of lemon hidden in the dough adds just a note of brightness to the cookies. I feel so fancy eating them, but they really aren't too difficult to make. The secret to the smooth jam filling is to heat the jam so that is will pour easily and then will set up into that smooth, almost glassy surface.

Yield: 16 cookies

DIRECTIONS:

1. Cream together the butter and sugar. Add the eggs and mix until combined. Add the baking powder, salt, xanthan gum, flavorings, and lemon zest and mix until combined.

2. Add the almond meal and GF Cookie Blend and mix until the dough is smooth.

3. Cover the dough and chill for at least 1 hour in the fridge. You may chill the dough up to 2-3 days but if you want to wait longer to bake the cookies I suggest storing the dough in the freezer and then letting it thaw in the fridge for several hours before rolling.

4. Preheat the oven to 350 degrees F. Line your baking sheets with parchment paper or silicone baking mats.

5. Divide the dough in half and roll the dough out between 2 sheets of plastic wrap until it is ¼ inch thick. Cut out with desired cookie cutters (I used 2–2½ inch rounds) , cutting a smaller shape out of exactly half of the cookies (that is for the jam to shine through) and place half and inch apart on a parchment or silicone baking mat lined baking sheet and bake for approximately 8 minutes. The cookie should have not yet turned golden around the edges, but will be slightly golden underneath and will have lost its doughy shine. They will still be soft

6. Cool on the baking sheet for a few minutes before moving to a cooling rack to cool.

7. To put the cookies together, warm the jam in the microwave (30 second increments, stirring in between) so that it is slightly melted, and very smooth. Spread a very thin layer on the top of the whole cookie (one without the cutout) and place a matching cookie with a cutout on top. Think of this like gluing the together. Repeat with the remaining cookies.

8. Dust all the cookies lightly with powdered sugar.

9. Load the remaining jam into a sandwich sized plastic bag and snip a little bit off of the corner. Pipe the jam into the center of the cookies where the cutout is, being careful not to let it spill over (I underfill mine just a tad to make them easier to handle.)

INGREDIENTS:

4 ounces (½ cup) butter, softened

2 ounces (¼ cup) white sugar

1 egg

½ teaspoon baking powder

¼ teaspoon salt

¼ teaspoon xanthan gum

¼ teaspoon vanilla

¼ teaspoon almond or lemon

zest of 1 lemon (about ½-1 teaspoon)

2.75 ounces (¾ cup) almond meal

8.25 ounces (1½ cup) GF Cookie Blend

½ cup raspberry (or other) jam

powdered sugar for dusting

Whoopie Pies

I hadn't ever had a traditional New England Whoopie Pie before, but I love these sweet chocolate cakey cookies, and I filled mine with creamy American Buttercream (see Chapter 7). I've been told these cookies aren't quite as thick as the traditional Whoopie Pie, if you like yours thicker just chill the batter before baking, which will prevent the cookies from spreading as much. Ta-da, thicker cookie!

Yield: 14 sandwiches

DIRECTIONS:

1. Preheat the oven to 350 degrees F. Line your baking sheets with parchment paper or silicone baking mats.

2. Cream together the butter and sugar. Add the eggs and mix until combined. Add the baking soda, baking powder, salt, xanthan gum, cocoa powder, and salt and mix until combined. While mixing add ⅓ of the GF Cookie Blend and then ⅓ of the milk alternating until you have added it all.

3. Drop the batter onto your prepared baking sheets using a 1½ tablespoon cookie scoop, 5 or 6 to a sheet (approximately 3 inches apart.)

4. Bake for 10 minutes. The cookie will be done when it loses its doughy shine, but it will still be soft if you touch it.

5. Cool for a few minutes on the baking sheet before moving to a cooling rack to finish cooling.

6. Frost the bottom of 1 cookie with *American Buttercream* (or marshmallow frosting) and top with a second cookie.

I recommend storing your sandwiches in the fridge in an airtight container once they are filled, 2-4 days. For longer storage pop them in the freezer.

INGREDIENTS:

4 ounces (½ cup) butter, softened

8 ounces (1 cup) white sugar

2 eggs

1½ teaspoon baking soda

¼ teaspoon baking powder

½ teaspoon xanthan gum

½ teaspoon salt

8.25 (1½ cups) GF Cookie Blend

2 ounces (½ cup) cocoa powder

1 cup buttermilk (or sour milk)

American Buttercream, page 139

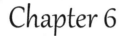

Chapter 6

Bar Cookies

....

Sugar Cookie Bars

* *

It can be a lot of work to rollout, cut, and frost a batch of sugar cookies. You get the same sugar cookie flavor and sweet creamy frosting but with just a fraction of the work.

Yield: 16 2" x 2" cookie bars Ingredients:

DIRECTIONS:

1. Preheat the oven to 350 degrees F. Line an 8" x 8" baking pan with parchment paper

2. Cream the butter and sugar together. Add the eggs and beat until combined.

3. Add the salt, baking powder, xanthan gum, and vanilla. Then add the GF Cookie Blend and mix until combined.

4. Press dough evenly into your prepared pan. Bake for 25-30 minutes or until a fork inserted near the center comes out clean, with only a few crumbs. The top of the bars will have lost their doughy shine.

5. Once the bars have cooled completely frost with colored *American Buttercream* and sprinkles.

Ingredients:

4 ounces (½ cup) butter, softened

4 ounces (½ cup) sugar

1 eggs

½ teaspoon salt

¾ teaspoon baking powder

¾ teaspoon xanthan gum

¾ teaspoon vanilla

9 ounces (1½ cups) GF Cookie Blend

1 recipe *American Buttercream*, page 139, colored with a few drops of food coloring (optional)

sprinkles (optional)

Chocolate Chip Bars

Sometimes even chocolate chip cookies seem like too much work. When that is the case, just make these bars; no need to dish out countless cookies and wash tons of baking sheets and cooling racks. 1 bowl, 1 pan, all the same taste.

Yield: 16 2" x 2" bars

Directions:

1. Preheat the oven to 350 degrees F. Line an 8" x 8" baking dish with parchment paper.

2. Cream together the melted butter and brown sugar on medium-low speed. Add the eggs and mix until combined. Add the baking powder, salt, xanthan gum, and vanilla and mix until combined.

3. Add the flour, and mix until incorporated. Then mix in the chocolate chips.

4. Press the dough evenly into the lined baking dish and bake for 28-30 minutes. When done the bars should be a little crinkly on the top and should have lost their doughy shine. They will still be very soft so it is important to cool all the way before cutting. You can speed this up by placing the bars in the fridge or in a cooler area (just don't place a glass baking dish in a cold place while it is still hot; it may shatter.)

Ingredients:

4 ounces (½ cup) butter, melted

5.5 ounces (½ cup + 3 tablespoon firmly packed) brown sugar

2 egg YOLKS

½ teaspoon xanthan gum

½ teaspoon baking powder

1 teaspoon vanilla

9 ounces (1.6 cup) GF Cookie Blend

6 ounces (⅞ cup) chocolate chips

Blondies

● ●

I remember making blondies with my mom when I was a girl. I found the concept very intriguing, a brownie without chocolate? However, since we loved chocolate so much we would always add some to the top. Right when the blondies came out of the oven we'd sprinkle them with chocolate chips and then once the chips were melted we'd spread the chocolate even.

Yield: 16 2" x 2" blondies

Directions:

1. Preheat oven to 350 degrees F. Line an 8" x 8" baking pan with parchment paper.

2. Mix the melted butter and brown sugar.

3. Add the xanthan gum, salt, vanilla, and egg and mix until combined. Add the GF Cookie Blend and mix until combined.

4. Pour the batter into the prepared pan and smooth out the top with a offset spatula, or knife.

5. Bake for 30-35 minutes or until a fork inserted near the center comes out mostly clean with only a few crumbs clinging to it.

6. Cool before cutting.

Ingredients:

2 ounces (¼ cup) butter, melted

6 ounces (¾ cup) brown sugar

1 egg

½ teaspoon xanthan gum

½ teaspoon salt

1 teaspoon vanilla

5.5 ounces (1 cup) GF Cookie Blend

Rocky Road Brownies

Rocky Road is such a fun, and in a way almost traditional, brownie topping. Crunchy almonds, gooey toasted marshmallows, and extra chocolate just for good measure; these brownies are sure to become a family favorite. (If desired you can use the dark chocolate brownie batter instead of the batter given. I love it both ways.)

Yield: 16 2" x 2" brownies

Directions:

1. Preheat the oven to 350 degrees F. Line an 8" x 8" baking dish with parchment paper

2. Beat the butter, sugar, and cocoa on medium-high speed until it is almost creamy.

3. Add the xanthan gum, salt, water, vanilla, and eggs and mix until combined. Add the GF Cookie Blend and mix until combined.

4. Pour the batter into the prepared pan and smooth out the top with a offset spatula, or knife.

5. Sprinkle the top of the brownies with the marshmallows, chocolate chips, and sliced almonds.

6. Bake for 30-35 minutes or until a fork inserted near the center comes out mostly clean with only a few crumbs clinging to it.

7. Cool before cutting.

Ingredients:

4 ounces (½ cup) butter, melted

10 ounces (1¼ cups) white sugar

3 ounces (¾ cup) cocoa powder

¼ teaspoon xanthan gum

¼ teaspoon salt

1½ tablespoons water

1 teaspoon vanilla

2 eggs

2.75 (½ cup) GF Cookie Blend

2 ounces (½ cup) sliced almonds

3.5 ounces (½ cup) chocolate chips

2 ounces (1 cup) mini marshmallows

Peanut Butter Swirl Brownies

Another one of my favorite childhood treats, whenever my dad made a box of brownies he would swirl in a few tablespoons of peanut butter. Peanut butter and chocolate are just made for each other, and are perfect together in these brownies. (If desired you can use the dark chocolate brownie batter instead of the batter given. I love it both ways.)

Yield: 16 2" x 2" brownies

Directions:

1. Preheat the oven to 350 degrees F. Line an 8" x 8" baking dish with parchment paper

2. In your stand mixer beat the butter, sugar, and cocoa on medium-high speed until it is almost creamy.

3. Add the xanthan gum, salt, water, vanilla, and eggs and mix until combined. Add the GF Cookie Blend and mix until combined.

4. Pour the batter into the prepared pan and smooth out the top with a offset spatula, or knife.

5. In a microwave safe bowl heat the peanut butter for 15 seconds at a time, stirring between heating, until it is smooth and spreads very easily. (30 seconds – 1 minute total, depending on your microwave.)

6. Drop spoonfuls of peanut butter on the top of the batter, 2-3 inches apart. Swirl by pulling a knife through the peanut butter, being careful to not mix the peanut butter into the batter, just a nice marble.

7. Bake for 30-35 minutes or until a fork inserted near the center comes out mostly clean with only a few crumbs clinging to it.

8. Cool before cutting.

Ingredients:

4 ounces (½ cup) butter, melted

10 ounces (1¼ cups) white sugar

3 ounces (¾ cup) cocoa powder

¼ teaspoon xanthan gum

¼ teaspoon salt

1½ tablespoons water

1 teaspoon vanilla

2 eggs

2.75 (½ cup) GF Cookie Blend

4.5 ounces (½ cup) natural peanut butter

Salted Caramel Praline Blondies

Salted caramel and pecans only make blondies better. Oozing with gooey caramel and studded with pecans; it doesn't get any better than that!

Yield: 16 2" x 2" blondies

DIRECTIONS:

1. Preheat oven to 350 degrees F. Line an 8" x 8" baking pan with parchment paper.

2. Mix the melted butter and brown sugar.

3. Add the xanthan gum, salt, vanilla, and egg and mix until combined. Add the GF Cookie Blend and mix until combined. Coarsely chop half the pecans and stir them into the batter.

4. Pour the batter into the prepared pan and smooth out the top with a offset spatula, or knife.

5. Drop the salted caramel by spoonfuls onto the batter, 2-3 inches apart. Drag a knife through the caramel, swirling it gently and being careful not to over mix it. Sprinkle the top with whole pecans.

6. Bake for 30-35 minutes or until a fork inserted near the center comes out mostly clean with only a few crumbs clinging to it.

7. Cool before cutting.

INGREDIENTS:

2 ounces (¼ cup) butter, melted

6 ounces (¾ cup) brown sugar

1 egg

½ teaspoon xanthan gum

½ teaspoon salt

1 teaspoon vanilla

5.5 ounces (1 cup) GF Cookie Blend

2 ounces (½ cup) whole pecans

¼ cup *Salted Caramel, page 145*

Boo Brownies

· ·

When I was a little girl my mom first came up with Boo Brownies. I know that cream cheese swirled brownies aren't really a new concept, but we made them for Halloween and named them Boo brownies because the swirls of cream cheese looked like little ghosts. (If desired you can use the dark chocolate brownie batter instead of the batter given. I love it both ways.)

Yield: 16 2" x 2" brownies

DIRECTIONS:

1. Preheat the oven to 350 degrees F. Line an 8" x 8" baking dish with parchment paper.

2. Beat the butter, sugar, and cocoa on medium-high speed until it is almost creamy.

3. Add the xanthan gum, salt, water, vanilla, and eggs and mix until combined. Add the GF Cookie Blend and mix until combined.

4. Pour the batter into the prepared pan and smooth out the top with a offset spatula, or knife.

5. In a small bowl with electric beaters beat together the cream cheese and sugar until smooth.

6. Drop spoonfuls on top of the batter 2-3 inches apart. Carefully swirl the cream cheese mixture by pulling a butter-knife through the cream cheese mixture several times. Be careful not to over mix it.

7. Bake for 30-35 minutes or until a fork inserted near the center comes out mostly clean with only a few crumbs clinging to it.

8. Cool before cutting.

INGREDIENTS:

4 ounces (½ cup) butter, melted

10 ounces (1¼ cups) white sugar

3 ounces (¾ cup) cocoa powder

¼ teaspoon xanthan gum

¼ teaspoon salt

1½ tablespoons water

1 teaspoon vanilla

2 eggs

2.75 (½ cup) GF Cookie Blend

4 ounces cream cheese, softened

2 tablespoons white sugar

Browned Butter Brownies

I love what browned butter does to these brownies; it gives them just a subtle nuttiness that accentuates the chocolate, making the brownies taste even richer.

Yield: **16 2" x 2" brownies**

DIRECTIONS:

1. Preheat the oven to 350 degrees F. Line an 8" x 8" baking dish with parchment paper

2. Melt the butter on medium to low heat. Continue to heat while stirring until the milk solids in the butter begin to brown. Watch it very carefully to make sure it doesn't burn. Allow the butter to cool slightly.

3. Beat the butter, sugar, and cocoa on medium-high speed until it is almost creamy.

4. Add the xanthan gum, salt, water, vanilla, and eggs and mix until combined. Add the GF Cookie Blend and mix until combined.

5. Pour the batter into the prepared pan and smooth out the top with a offset spatula, or knife.

6. Bake for 30-35 minutes or until a fork inserted near the center comes out mostly clean with only a few crumbs clinging to it.

7. Cool before cutting

INGREDIENTS:

4 ounces (½ cup) butter

10 ounces (1¼ cups) white sugar

3 ounces (¾ cup) cocoa powder

¼ teaspoon xanthan gum

¼ teaspoon salt

1½ tablespoons water

1 teaspoon vanilla

2 eggs

2.75 (½ cup) GF Cookie Blend

Dark Chocolate Brownies

My husband is a brownie snob. His perfect brownie has to be fudgy while still having a nice crumb and bite, and it can't be too rich. He doesn't like my browned butter brownies, they are too rich for him and not chewy enough. (I still love them though!) I made many different batches, trying lots of different ingredients, to come up with a brownie that my husband would like. This is the recipe that I developed for him, and then sold them at local farmer's markets. Using melted chocolate instead of cocoa powder really makes these brownies have the perfect flavor and texture.

Yield: 16 2" x 2" brownies

DIRECTIONS:

1. Preheat the oven to 350 degrees F. Line an 9" x 13" pan with parchment paper.

2. In a saucepan over med – low heat melt together the chocolate and oil. Remove from heat and let cool slightly.

3. Stir in the sugar, and then the almond meal, GF Cookie Blend, and salt.

4. Stir in the eggs one at a time.

5. Stir in the remaining chocolate chips.

6. Spread the batter into the prepared pan and bake for approximately 30 minutes or until a toothpick inserted near the center comes out mostly clean, with just a few moist crumbs clinging to it.

7. Let cool before cutting so that the brownies have a chance to set up.

INGREDIENTS:

10 ounces (approximately 1¼ cups) bittersweet or semisweet chocolate

½ cup vegetable oil (or 8 ounces butter, melted)

5 ounces (1¼ cups) almond flour/meal

3.2 ounces (½ cup) GF Cookie Blend

12 ounces (1½ cups) sugar

1 teaspoon salt

4 eggs

4 ounces (½ cup) chocolate chips

Blueberry Cream Cheese Bars

I am a blueberry-loving fiend some days. I love the combination of sweet blueberries and creamy cheese with a basic sugar cookie dough. All the flavors come together in these tasty bar cookies.

Yield: 16 2" x 2" Cookies

Directions:

1. Preheat oven to 350 degrees F. Line an 8" x 8" baking pan with parchment paper.

2. Cream together the butter and sugar. Add the egg and mix until smooth.

3. Add the baking powder, salt, and xanthan gum. Add the GF Cookie Blend and mix until combined. The dough will be very stiff.

4. Press ⅔ of the dough into the bottom of the prepared 8" x 8" pan.

5. Rinse and drain the blueberries. Toss in the flour and sugar and sprinkle over the dough.

6. Cut the cream cheese into ½ inch cubes and sprinkle over the blueberries.

7. Break/crumble the remaining ⅓ dough over the top of the blueberries and cream cheese.

8. Bake for 20-25 minutes or until the cookie dough loses its shine and a fork inserted in the middle comes out clean (except blueberry and cream cheese.)

9. Let cool before cutting.

Ingredients:

9.6 ounces (1¾ cup) GF Cookie Blend

2 ounces (¼ cup) butter, softened

1 egg

½ teaspoon baking powder

¼ teaspoon salt

½ teaspoon xanthan gum

4 ounces (½ cup) sugar

1 cup blueberries

1 tablespoon flour Blend

1 tablespoon sugar

4 ounces cream cheese

Peanut Butter Chocolate Bars

*When I was a little girl we'd often have Sunday dinner at my aunt's house. She loved to bake, and these bars were one of my favorite treats that she'd make. The cookie base is packed with peanut butter flavor, but what really makes these special is the peanut butter frosting that melts on the top. Finish it off with a smooth layer of **Chocolate Ganache** (Chapter 7). It doesn't get any better.*

Directions:

1. Preheat the oven to 350 degrees F. Line a 9" x 13" baking sheet with parchment paper.

2. Cream the sugars and butter. Add the eggs and vanilla and mix until smooth. Add the peanut butter and mix until combined. Stir in the baking soda, salt, GF Cookie Blend, and GF oats, and xanthan gum.

3. Spread evenly in the prepared pan. Bake for 12-15 minutes.

4. While the cookies bake, mix together the all the frosting ingredients until smooth. Frost the bars when they are still warm.

5. Once they are completely cooled top with *Chocolate Ganache,* or your favorite chocolate frosting.

Ingredients:

4 ounces (½ cup) white sugar

4 ounces (½ cup firmly packed) brown sugar

4 ounces (½ cup) butter, softened

1 egg

½ teaspoon vanilla

⅓ cup peanut butter

½ teaspoon baking soda

¼ teaspoon salt

5.5 ounces (1 cup) GF Cookie Blend

4 ounces (1 cup) GF rolled oats

¼ teaspoon of xanthan gum

Frosting:

2 ounces (½ cup) powdered sugar

¼ cup peanut butter

1 tablespoon milk

Chocolate Ganache, page 138

Peanut Butter Banana Blondies

The mom of one of my little sister's friends brought us Peanut Butter Banana Blondies when I was a little girl. I love how the flavors of the sweet bananas and nutty peanut butter mingle in these yummy bars. Next time you have a bunch of ripe bananas sitting on your counter, this recipe is a great way to use them!

Yield: 16 2" x 2" blondies

Directions:

1. Preheat the oven to 350 degrees F. Line an 8" x 8" baking pan with parchment paper.

2. Sift together the GF Cookie Blend, baking powder, salt, and xanthan gum.

3. Cream together the butter, peanut butter, and banana. Add the sugar and eggs and mix until combined.

4. Add the sifted flour mix and mix until combined. Stir in the chocolate chips.

5. Bake for 35-40 minutes or until a toothpick inserted in the middle of the pan comes out clean with only a few crumbs.

6. Let cool before cutting.

Ingredients:

5.5 ounces (1 cup) GF Cookie Blend

1½ teaspoon baking powder

¼ teaspoon salt

½ teaspoon xanthan gum

2.6 ounces (⅓ cup) butter, softened

4.5 ounces (½ cup) all natural peanut butter

½ - ¾ cup mashed banana (about 2 bananas)

4 ounces (½ cup) brown sugar

2 ounces (¼ cup) white sugar

2 eggs

6 ounces (¾ cup) chocolate chips

Lemon Bars

I've always been a sucker for a good lemon bar; sweet buttery shortbread topped with tart lemon curd and all sprinkled in powdered sugar. The problem I always had with gluten-free lemon bars was the crust, it usually crumbled to bits when baking/eating. My secret is to use some egg white in the shortbread dough, it adds just enough structure to keep the crust together, but it still retains its buttery, crispy texture. Don't skip the lemon zest! That is where most of the bright lemon flavor comes from.

Yield: 15 approximately 3" squares

DIRECTIONS:

1. Preheat the oven to 350 degrees F. Line a 9" x 13" pan with parchment paper, or lightly grease.

2. Cream together the butter and sugar, mix in the egg white. Add the GF Cookie Blend, xanthan gum, and salt and mix until you have a smooth dough.

3. Press the dough into the bottom of the prepared pan. Bake for 15-20 minutes or until it is set and slightly golden around the edges.

4. Meanwhile, start on the filling by whisking together the eggs and sugar. Add the lemon juice, zest, and GF Cookie Blend.

5. Pour the filling over the baked crust and bake for an additional 20-25 minutes or until the edges are set and the center jiggles slightly if you shake the pan. The cookies will set up more as they cool.

6. Cut into squares and just before serving dust with powdered sugar.

INGREDIENTS:

CRUST:

2 ounces (½ cup) powdered sugar

4 ounces (½ cup) butter, softened

1 egg white

8.25 ounces (1½ cups) GF Cookie Blend

¼ teaspoon xgum

¼ teaspoon salt

LEMON FILLING:

6 eggs

16 ounces (2 cups) white sugar

2 ounces (¼ cup plus 2 tablespoons) GF Cookie Blend

Zest and juice from 3 lemons (about ½ cup lemon juice)

additional powdered sugar for dusting

Vegan Black Bean Brownies

Wonderfully gooey, these brownies have a beautifully crisp outer edge and deep chocolatey flavour. The black beans add density to the brownies yet lend their natural, velvety texture to add a new dimension of smoothness to each bite. The beans and flax meal give these brownies extra fiber to make these brownies a little bit healthier.

DIRECTIONS:

1. Preheat oven to 350 degrees F. Line a 8" x 8" baking dish with parchment paper (to get the paper to stick, dab some oil on the sides and in the middle) .

2. In a bowl, combine flax meal and warm water and let sit until thickened.

3. In a food processor, purée the black beans until smooth. Add in coconut oil, flax meal, cocoa powder, vanilla, white sugar, and ¼ cup chocolate chips and process until incorporated.

4. Pour the batter into the lined baking pan, and spread evenly. Sprinkle the remaining ¼ cup of chocolate chips on top, and bake for 35-40 minutes until the middle is set (when you jostle the pan, it won't jiggle. Alternatively, you can stick a toothpick in the middle to see if it comes out clean)

5. Let the brownies cool *completely* in the pan on a wire rack. Run a sharp knife around the edges to release the brownies and pull on the sides of parchment paper to put them on a cutting board. Using a sharp knife, cut into 16 squares. Enjoy within 2-4 days, storing the brownies in the fridge in an airtight container and separating the layers with parchment paper.

Lisa Le, Je suis alimentageuse

INGREDIENTS:

3 tablespoon flax meal

¾ cup warm water

1 can (19 fluid ounces) black beans, rinsed and drained

3 tablespoon coconut oil

2 ounces (½ cup) cocoa powder

1 teaspoon vanilla

5.3 ounces (⅔ cup) white sugar

½ cup dairy-free chocolate chips (divided ¼ and ¼ cup)

Chapter 7

Frostings & Fillings

American Buttercream

DIRECTIONS:

1. In the bowl of your stand mixer beat the butter on medium-high until light in color and fluffy, 3-5 minutes.

2. Add the powdered sugar, 1 tablespoon cream, and vanilla and beat until combined—low speed at first so that you don't fling powdered sugar all over the kitchen. If the frosting looks too dry or is a bit too stiff add more cream, a tablespoon at a time, until the frosting is at the desired consistency (up to 3 tablespoons of cream total.) Increase the speed to medium-high and beat for another 2-3 minutes. Stir in a tiny bit of gel food coloring, if desired.

3. Use to fill whoopies pies, or frost sugar cookies and all your other favorites.

For frosting or filling cookies:

Using a rubber scraper/spatula load the frosting into a piping bag fitted with a large round tip. Hold the tip perpendicular to the cookie and pipe a layer of frosting, starting at the edge and going around in a circular pattern without overlapping until you are in the center. For frosting, smooth out the frosting with a small offset spatula and top with some sprinkles. For filling, just place another cookie on top.

Ingredients:

4 ounces (½ cup) butter, softened

8 ounces (2 cups) powdered sugar

1 teaspoon vanilla

1-3 tablespoons heavy cream

Ingredients:

2 cups bittersweet, semisweet, or milk chocolate chips

¾ cup cream

Chocolate Ganache

· ·

DIRECTIONS:

1. Coarsely chop any large pieces of chocolate (regular sized chips are fine just the way they are.) Place the chocolate in a mixing bowl.

2. Heat the cream either in a saucepan over medium heat or in a microwave safe bowl, heating for 30 second increments, until it is steaming and just starting to make tiny bubbles around the edges.

3. Immediately pour the cream over the chocolate and stir until the chocolate is all melted and smooth.

4. Allow to cool to just above room temperature before using.

Marshmallow Fluff Filling

. . . .

Ingredients:

4 egg whites

12 ounces (1½ cup)
White sugar, plus 1
tablespoon

½ cup water

4 ounces (1 cup)
powdered sugar
(optional)

DIRECTIONS:

1. To make the filling, stir together 1½ cups sugar and the water in a heavy-bottomed medium saucepan and heat over medium high heat until the sugar reaches approximately 230 degrees F. (soft ball stage) It will be clear, all the sugar will dissolve, and the syrup will thicken. If you were to drop a small amount of the syrup into ice water it would solidify into a soft ball that would bounce when removed from the ice water. It should take 5-7 minutes to reach this stage once it starts to bubble.

2. While the sugar is cooking, whip the egg whites in a stand mixer until they are foamy. Add the remaining 1 tablespoon of sugar and whip until the egg whites reach soft-medium peaks. (if the egg whites reach soft-medium peaks before they syrup is ready just turn off the mixer and wait for the syrup.)

3. Once the syrup has reached 230 degrees F. (softball stage) turn the stand mixer on low speed and slowly pour the syrup into the egg whites in a slow and steady stream. Turn the speed up to medium-high speed and beat until the mixture is cool to the touch.

4. You can use the Marshmallow Fluff as is, or if desired beat in an additional 4 ounces (1 cup) of powdered sugar to thicken it and make it more frosting like.

Cream Cheese Frosting

Ingredients:

4 ounces cream cheese, softened

2 ounces butter, softened

16 ounces (4 cups) powdered sugar

2 tablespoons heavy whipping cream

1 teaspoon vanilla

DIRECTIONS:

1. Whip butter and cream cheese in a stand mixer (or using heavy duty electric beaters) on medium-high speed for 5 minutes. It will become very pale in color and airy.

2. Add the powdered sugar, vanilla, and cream while beating on low, and then turn the speed back up and beat for an additional 3 minutes.

3. Use to fill red velvet sandwich cookies, or to fill or frost any other cookie.

German Chocolate Frosting

Ingredients:

8 ounces (1 cup) white sugar

¾ cup milk

2 ounces (¼ cup) butter

3 eggs

4.25 (1⅓ cup) shredded coconut

4 ounces (1 cup) chopped pecans

1 teaspoon vanilla

DIRECTIONS:

1. To make the frosting whisk together the milk, eggs, sugar, butter, and vanilla over medium low heat until it thickens (whisk continuously until you remove it from the heat to prevent the eggs from scrambling.)

2. Remove from heat and stir in the coconut and pecans.

Royal Icing

Ingredients:

1 egg white

3 ounces (¾ cup) powdered sugar

½ teaspoon vanilla or other extract

DIRECTIONS:

1. In a stand mixer, or bowl with electric beaters, mix the egg white until it is foamy. Add the powdered sugar 1oz (¼ c) at a time and continue to whip until it is thick and shiny (you may need more or less, depending on the weather. Test a little bit on a cookie to make sure it holds it shape. If it doesn't add more powdered sugar)

2. Load the frosting into a small sandwich bag. Squeeze out the air and seal it, then cut a small bit off of the corner and use it to decorate cookies. If desired sprinkle with sprinkles while the frosting is still wet. Allow to air dry for several hours before stacking the cookies.

Salted Caramel

. . . .

Ingredients:

4 ounces (½ cup) sugar

1 teaspoon vanilla extract or lemon juice

½ cup heavy cream

½-1 teaspoon salt, to taste

DIRECTIONS:

1. In a heavy bottomed saucepan mix together the sugar and extract or lemon juicee. It will look like wet sand.

2. Cook over medium heat until the sugar begins to melt. Continue to stir continually until the sugar browns and melts completely.

3. Add the cream and continue to stir until the sugar and cream melt together and the mixture are smooth. It will bubble and the sugar may harden, but if you continue to heat and stir it it should all melt together, it just takes patience. If there are any remaining large clumps of hardened sugar pour the caramel through a sieve.

4. Salt to taste, start with ½ tsp and then add more as desired.

Ingredients:

6 ounces (1½ cup) powdered sugar

½ teaspoon vanilla extract

2 ounces (¼ cup) shortening

1 tablespoon water, hot

Vanilla Crème Filling

DIRECTIONS:

1. In a stand mixer (or with heavy duty electric beaters) whip the shortening until it becomes fluffy (about 5 minutes.) Add the powdered sugar, vanilla, and hot water and continue to beat until you have a smooth frosting.

2, The easiest way to fill cookies with this oreo-style filling is to fill a piping bag, or plastic sandwich or gallon sized bag, with the filling. If you are using a plastic bag snip the tip off of one of the corners. Pipe a circle of frosting in the center of the bottom of one cookie. Place another cookie on top and squeeze slightly to press the filling out to the edges.

Index

Resources

· ·

Looking for more resources for baking tips and ideas? These are our favorite resources. Some of our ideas have come from cookbooks that aren't gluten-free, so we're including any references that we've found helpful. Check out some of these websites and books. Enjoy!

Books:

Artisanal Gluten-Free Cupcakes by Kelli and Peter Bronski

Beyond the Moon Cookbook by Ginny Callan

Cooking for Isaiah: Gluten-Free and Dairy-Free Recipes for Easy, Delicious Meals by Silvana Nardone

Everyday Raw Desserts by Mathew Kenney

Gluten-Free Baking for Dummies by Dr. Jean McFadden Layton and Linda Larsen

Gluten-Free Makeovers by Beth Hillson

Gluten-Free on a Shoestring by Nicole Hunn

Gluten-Free Quick & Easy by Carol Fenster

Go Dairy Free by Alisa Marie Fleming

Good Morning: Breakfasts without Gluten, Sugar, Eggs or Dairy by Ricki Heller

How Baking Works by Paula Figoni

Kids Can Cook by Dorothy R. Bates

The Flavor Bible: The Essential Guide to Culinary Creativity, Based on the Wisdom of America's Most Imaginative Chefs by Karen Page and Andrew Dornenburg

The Gluten-Free Almond Flour Cookbook by Elana Amsterdam

The Gluten-Free Gourmet: Living Well Without Wheat by Bette Hagman

The Spunky Coconut Cookbook by Kelly Brozyna

Magazines:

Gluten-Free Living
www.glutenfreeliving.com

Easy Eats
www.easyeats.com

Living Without
www.livingwithout.com

Fine Cooking
www.finecooking.com

Blogs and Websites:

Adventures of a Gluten-Free Mom
www.adventuresofaglutenfreemom.com

Affairs of Living
www.affairsofliving.com

Book of Yum
www.bookofyum.com/blog

Celiac Teen
www.celiacteen.com

Chocolate Covered Katie
www.chocolatecoveredkatie.com

Choosing Raw
www.choosingraw.com

Cook it Allergy Free
www.cookitallergyfree.com

Diet, Dessert, and Dogs
www.dietdessertndogs.com

Eat Good 4 Life
http://www.eatgood4life.com/

Elana's Pantry
www.elanaspantry.com

Ginger Lemon Girl
www.gingerlemongirl.blogspot.com

Gluten-Free Easily
www.glutenfreeeasily.com

Gluten-Free Gigi
www.glutenfreegigi.com

Gluten-Free Goddess
www.glutenfreegoddess.blogspot.com

Gluten Free on a Shoestring
www.glutenfreeonashoestring.com

Jenn Cuisine
www.jenncuisine.com

Je suis alimentegeuse
http://alimentageuse.com/home/

Just Me, Gluten – Free
Frugal Antics of a Harried Homemaker
http://frugalanticsrecipes.com/
http://justmeglutenfree.com

Karina's Kitchen
www.glutenfreegoddess.blogspot.com

Pure 2 Raw
www.pure2raw.com

Manifest Vegan
www.manifestvegan.com

Sally's Baking Addiction
http://sallysbakingaddiction.com/

She Let Them Eat Cake
www.sheletthemeatcake.com

Silvana's Kitchen
www.silvanaskitchen.com

Simply Sugar & Gluten-Free
www.simplysugarandglutenfree.com

Simply … Gluten-Free
www.simplygluten-free.com

Straight into Bed Cakefree and Dried
www.milkforthemorningcake.blogspot.
com

Tasty Eats at Home
www.tastyeatsathome.com

The W.H.O.L.E. Gang
www.thewholegang.org

Tortillas and Honey
http://www.tortillasandhoney.com/

Triumph Dining Blog
http://www.triumphdining.com/
blog/2013/12/15/cookie-exchange-
triumph-dining-holiday-week/

Whole Life Nutrition Kitchen
www.nourishingmeals.com

The Balanced Platter
www.balancedplatter.com

The Mommy Bowl
www.themommybowl.com

The Spunky Coconut
www.thespunkycoconut.com

Z's Cup of Tea
www.zscupoftea.com